Books by Anthony Hecht

POETRY

The Transparent Man   1990
Collected Earlier Poems   1990
The Venetian Vespers   1979
Millions of Strange Shadows   1977
The Hard Hours   1967
A Summoning of Stones   1954

TRANSLATION

Aeschylus's Seven Against Thebes   1973
(WITH HELEN BACON)

ESSAYS

Obbligati   1986

COLLECTED EARLIER POEMS

THE COMPLETE TEXTS OF

THE HARD HOURS

MILLIONS OF STRANGE SHADOWS

THE VENETIAN VESPERS

COLLECTED
EARLIER
POEMS

ANTHONY
HECHT

Alfred A. Knopf   *New York*   1990

THIS IS A BORZOI BOOK
PUBLISHED BY ALFRED A. KNOPF, INC.

Originally published in 3 volumes by Atheneum Publishers.

The Hard Hours: Copyright 1948, 1949, 1950, 1951, 1952, 1953, 1954, © 1955, 1956, 1957, 1958, 1959, 1960, 1961, 1962, 1963, 1964, 1965, 1966, 1967 by Anthony E. Hecht

Millions of Strange Shadows: Copyright © 1977 by Anthony E. Hecht

The Venetian Vespers: Copyright © 1979 by Anthony E. Hecht

Poems from these 3 volumes were originally published in the following:

The American Scholar, Antaeus, Book Week, Botteghe Oscure, Encounter, Georgia Review, Harpers, Harpers Bazaar, Harvard Advocate, Hudson Review, Kenyon Review, Marxist Perspectives, The Nation, New American Review, The New Leader, The New Republic, New Statesman, The New Yorker, The Noble Savage, Partisan Review, Ploughshares, Poetry, Quarterly Review of Literature, Times Literary Supplement, Transatlantic Review, Voices, and *Wild Places.*

"The Seven Deadly Sins" and "Improvisations on Aesop" were originally published by The Gehenna Press, with wood engravings by Leonard Baskin.

Acknowledgment to George Dimock, Jr., and William Arrowsmith for assistance in translating the chorus from Sophocles' *Oedipus at Kolonos.*

The translation of Voltaire's "Poem Upon the Lisbon Disaster" originally appeared in a limited edition published by The Penmaen Press.

"Green: An Epistle" was the Phi Beta Kappa poem for Swarthmore in 1971; "The Odds" was the Phi Beta Kappa poem for Harvard in 1975.

"The Venetian Vespers" appeared first in book form in a limited edition published by David R. Godine. Copyright © 1979 by Anthony E. Hecht.

The versions of the two poems of Joseph Brodsky were made for his book of poems, *A Part of Speech,* published by Farrar, Straus & Giroux, Inc., 1980. Copyright © 1979 by Farrar, Straus & Giroux, Inc.

Library of Congress Cataloging-in-Publication Data

    Hecht, Anthony
      [Poems]
      Collected earlier poems : the complete texts of The hard hours, Millions of strange shadows, The Venetian vespers / Anthony Hecht. —1st ed.
      p. cm.
      ISBN 0-394-58505-4
      I. Title.
PS3558.E28A17   1990   89-43356
811'54—dc20   CIP

CONTENTS

THE HARD HOURS

A HILL	2
THIRD AVENUE IN SUNLIGHT	4
TARANTULA, OR, THE DANCE OF DEATH	5
THE END OF THE WEEKEND	6
MESSAGE FROM THE CITY	7
JASON	9
BEHOLD THE LILIES OF THE FIELD	10
PIG	13
OSTIA ANTICA	14
THE DOVER BITCH	17
TO A MADONNA (*after Baudelaire*)	18
CLAIRE DE LUNE	20
THREE PROMPTERS FROM THE WINGS	22
LIZARDS AND SNAKES	30
ADAM	31
THE ORIGIN OF CENTAURS	33
THE VOW	
HEUREUX QUI, COMME ULYSSE, A FAIT UN BEAU VOYAGE (*after du Bellay*)	37
RITES AND CEREMONIES	38
A LETTER	48
THE SEVEN DEADLY SINS	49
UPON THE DEATH OF GEORGE SANTAYANA	56
BIRDWATCHERS OF AMERICA	57
THE SONG OF THE FLEA	58
THE MAN WHO MARRIED MAGDALENE (*Variations on a Theme by Louis Simpson*)	59
IMPROVISATIONS ON AESOP	61
THE THOUGHTFUL ROISTERER DECLINES THE GAMBIT (*after Charles Vion De Dalibray*)	62
GIANT TORTOISE	63
"MORE LIGHT! MORE LIGHT!"	64
"AND CAN YE SING BALULOO WHEN THE BAIRN GREETS?"	66
"IT OUT-HERODS HEROD. PRAY YOU, AVOID IT."	67

From A SUMMONING OF STONES

DOUBLE SONNET   71

LA CONDITION BOTANIQUE   72

JAPAN   76

LE MASSEUR DE MA SOEUR   79

AS PLATO SAID   81

DISCOURSE CONCERNING TEMPTATION   83

SAMUEL SEWALL   84

DRINKING SONG   85

A POEM FOR JULIA   86

CHRISTMAS IS COMING   89

IMITATION   91

THE GARDENS OF THE VILLA D'ESTE   92

A DEEP BREATH AT DAWN   97

A ROMAN HOLIDAY   100

ALCESTE IN THE WILDERNESS   102

MILLIONS OF STRANGE SHADOWS

THE COST	107
BLACK BOY IN THE DARK	110
AN AUTUMNAL	112
"DICHTUNG UND WAHRHEIT"	113
A VOICE AT A SEANCE	116
GREEN: AN EPISTLE	117
SOMEBODY'S LIFE	122
A LOT OF NIGHT MUSIC	123
A BIRTHDAY POEM	125
RETREAT	128
COMING HOME	129
PRAISE FOR KOLONOS	132
SESTINA D'INVERNO	134
ROME	136
SWAN DIVE	137
"AUGURIES OF INNOCENCE"	139
PERIPETEIA	140
AFTER THE RAIN	143
APPLES FOR PAUL SUTTMAN	145
THE HUNT	147
EXILE	149
THE FEAST OF STEPHEN	150
THE ODDS	152
APPREHENSIONS	154
THE GHOST IN THE MARTINI	160
GOING THE ROUNDS	164
GOLIARDIC SONG	167
"GLADNESS OF THE BEST"	168
POEM UPON THE LISBON DISASTER	170
FIFTH AVENUE PARADE	177
THE LULL	178

THE VENETIAN VESPERS

I

THE GRAPES   185

THE DEODAND   188

THE SHORT END   191

INVECTIVE AGAINST DENISE, A WITCH   204

AUSPICES   207

APPLICATION FOR A GRANT   208

AN OVERVIEW   209

STILL LIFE   211

PERSISTENCES   212

A CAST OF LIGHT   214

HOUSE SPARROWS   215

AN OLD MALEDICTION   217

II

THE VENETIAN VESPERS   221

III

Poems of Joseph Brodsky, versions by Anthony Hecht

CAPE COD LULLABY   251

LAGOON   266

NOTES   271

THE HARD HOURS

For my sons, JASON *and* ADAM

Were is that lawhing and that song
That trayling and that proude gong,
Tho havekes and tho houndes?
Al that joye is went away,
That wele is comen to weylaway,
To manye harde stoundes.

A HILL

In Italy, where this sort of thing can occur,
I had a vision once—though you understand
It was nothing at all like Dante's, or the visions of saints,
And perhaps not a vision at all. I was with some friends,
Picking my way through a warm sunlit piazza
In the early morning. A clear fretwork of shadows
From huge umbrellas littered the pavement and made
A sort of lucent shallows in which was moored
A small navy of carts. Books, coins, old maps,
Cheap landscapes and ugly religious prints
Were all on sale. The colors and noise
Like the flying hands were gestures of exultation,
So that even the bargaining
Rose to the ear like a voluble godliness.
And then, when it happened, the noises suddenly stopped,
And it got darker; pushcarts and people dissolved
And even the great Farnese Palace itself
Was gone, for all its marble; in its place
Was a hill, mole-colored and bare. It was very cold,
Close to freezing, with a promise of snow.
The trees were like old ironwork gathered for scrap
Outside a factory wall. There was no wind,
And the only sound for a while was the little click
Of ice as it broke in the mud under my feet.
I saw a piece of ribbon snagged on a hedge,
But no other sign of life. And then I heard
What seemed the crack of a rifle. A hunter, I guessed;
At least I was not alone. But just after that
Came the soft and papery crash
Of a great branch somewhere unseen falling to earth.

And that was all, except for the cold and silence
That promised to last forever, like the hill.

Then prices came through, and fingers, and I was restored
To the sunlight and my friends. But for more than a week

I was scared by the plain bitterness of what I had seen.
All this happened about ten years ago,
And it hasn't troubled me since, but at last, today,
I remembered that hill; it lies just to the left
Of the road north of Poughkeepsie; and as a boy
I stood before it for hours in wintertime.

THIRD AVENUE IN SUNLIGHT

Third Avenue in sunlight. Nature's error.
Already the bars are filled and John is there.
Beneath a plentiful lady over the mirror
He tilts his glass in the mild mahogany air.

I think of him when he first got out of college,
Serious, thin, unlikely to succeed;
For several months he hung around the Village,
Boldly T-shirted, unfettered but unfreed.

Now he confides to a stranger, "I was first scout,
And kept my glimmers peeled till after dark.
Our outfit had as its sign a bloody knout,
We met behind the museum in Central Park.

Of course, we were kids." But still those savages,
War-painted, a flap of leather at the loins,
File silently against him. Hostages
Are never taken. One summer, in Des Moines,

They entered his hotel room, tomahawks
Flashing like barracuda. He tried to pray.
Three years of treatment. Occasionally he talks
About how he almost didn't get away.

Daily the prowling sunlight whets its knife
Along the sidewalk. We almost never meet.
In the Rembrandt dark he lifts his amber life.
My bar is somewhat further down the street.

TARANTULA or THE DANCE OF DEATH

During the plague I came into my own.
It was a time of smoke-pots in the house
Against infection. The blind head of bone
           Grinned its abuse

Like a good democrat at everyone.
Runes were recited daily, charms were applied.
That was the time I came into my own.
           Half Europe died.

The symptoms are a fever and dark spots
First on the hands, then on the face and neck,
But even before the body, the mind rots.
           You can be sick

Only a day with it before you're dead.
But the most curious part of it is the dance.
The victim goes, in short, out of his head.
           A sort of trance

Glazes the eyes, and then the muscles take
His will away from him, the legs begin
Their funeral jig, the arms and belly shake
           Like souls in sin.

Some, caught in these convulsions, have been known
To fall from windows, fracturing the spine.
Others have drowned in streams. The smooth head-stone,
           The box of pine,

Are not for the likes of these. Moreover, flame
Is powerless against contagion.
That was the black winter when I came
           Into my own.

THE END OF THE WEEKEND

A dying firelight slides along the quirt
Of the cast-iron cowboy where he leans
Against my father's books. The lariat
Whirls into darkness. My girl, in skin-tight jeans,
Fingers a page of Captain Marryat,
Inviting insolent shadows to her shirt.

We rise together to the second floor.
Outside, across the lake, an endless wind
Whips at the headstones of the dead and wails
In the trees for all who have and have not sinned.
She rubs against me and I feel her nails.
Although we are alone, I lock the door.

The eventual shapes of all our formless prayers,
This dark, this cabin of loose imaginings,
Wind, lake, lip, everything awaits
The slow unloosening of her underthings.
And then the noise. Something is dropped. It grates
Against the attic beams.
      I climb the stairs,

Armed with a belt.
     A long magnesium strip
Of moonlight from the dormer cuts a path
Among the shattered skeletons of mice.
A great black presence beats its wings in wrath.
Above the boneyard burn its golden eyes.
Some small grey fur is pulsing in its grip.

MESSAGE FROM THE CITY

It is raining here.
On my neighbor's fire escape
geraniums are set out
in their brick-clay pots,
along with the mop,
old dishrags, and a cracked
enamel bowl for the dog.

I think of you out there
on the sandy edge of things,
rain strafing the beach,
the white maturity
of bones and broken shells,
and little tin shovels and cars
rusting under the house.

And between us there is—what?
Love and constraint,
conditions, conditions,
and several hundred miles
of billboards, filling-stations,
and little dripping gardens.
The fir tree full of whispers,
trinkets of water,
the bob, duck, and release
of the weighted rose,
life in the freshened stones.
(They used to say that rain
is good for growing boys,
and once I stood out in it
hoping to rise a foot.
The biggest drops fattened
on the gutters under the eaves,
sidled along the slant,
picked up speed, let go,
and met their dooms in a "plock"

beside my gleaming shins.
I must have been near the size
of your older son.)

Yesterday was nice.
I took my boys to the park.
We played Ogre on the grass.
I am, of course, the Ogre,
and invariably get killed.
Merciless and barefooted,
they sneak up from behind
and they let me have it.

O my dear, my dear,
today the rain pummels
the sour geraniums
and darkens the grey pilings
of your house, built upon sand.
And both of us, full grown,
have weathered a long year.
Perhaps your casual glance
will settle from time to time
on the sea's travelling muscles
that flex and roll their strength
under its rain-pocked skin.
And you'll see where the salt winds
have blown bare the seaward side
of the berry bushes,
and will notice
the faint, fresh
smell of iodine.

JASON

And from America the golden fleece   MARLOWE

The room is full of gold.
Is it a chapel? Is that the genuine buzz
Of cherubim, the wingèd goods?
Is it no more than sun that floods
To pool itself at her uncovered breast?
O lights, o numina, behold
How we are gifted. He who never was,
Is, and her fingers bless him and are blessed.

That blessedness is tossed
In a wild, dodging light. Suddenly clear
And poised in heavenly desire
Prophets and eastern saints take fire
And fuse with gold in windows across the way,
And turn to liquid, and are lost.
And now there deepens over lakes of air
A remembered stillness of the seventh day

Borne in on the soft cruise
And sway of birds. Slowly the ancient seas,
Those black, predestined waters rise
Lisping and calm before my eyes,
And Massachusetts rises out of foam
A state of mind in which by twos
All beasts browse among barns and apple trees
As in their earliest peace, and the dove comes home.

Tonight, my dear, when the moon
Settles the radiant dust of every man,
Powders the bedsheets and the floor
With lightness of those gone before,
Sleep then, and dream the story as foretold:
Dream how a little boy alone
With a wooden sword and the top of a garbage can
Triumphs in gardens full of marigold.

9

BEHOLD THE LILIES OF THE FIELD

for Leonard Baskin

And now. An attempt.
Don't tense yourself; take it easy.
Look at the flowers there in the glass bowl.
Yes, they are lovely and fresh. I remember
Giving my mother flowers once, rather like those
(Are they narcissus or jonquils?)
And I hoped she would show some pleasure in them
But got that mechanical enthusiastic show
She used on the telephone once in praising some friend
For thoughtfulness or good taste or whatever it was,
And when she hung up, turned to us all and said,
"God, what a bore she is!"
I think she was trying to show us how honest she was,
At least with us. But the effect
Was just the opposite, and now I don't think
She knows what honesty is. "Your mother's a whore,"
Someone said, not meaning she slept around,
Though perhaps this was part of it, but
Meaning she had lost all sense of honor,
And I think this is true.

But that's not what I wanted to say.
What was it I wanted to say?
When he said that about Mother, I had to laugh,
I really did, it was so amazingly true.
Where was I?
Lie back. Relax.
Oh yes. I remember now what it was.
It was what I saw them do to the emperor.
They captured him, you know. Eagles and all.
They stripped him, and made an iron collar for his neck,
And they made a cage out of our captured spears,
And they put him inside, naked and collared,
And exposed to the view of the whole enemy camp.
And I was tied to a post and made to watch

When he was taken out and flogged by one of their generals
And then forced to offer his ripped back
As a mounting block for the barbarian king
To get on his horse;
And one time to get down on all fours to be the royal throne
When the king received our ambassadors
To discuss the question of ransom.
Of course, he didn't want ransom.
And I was tied to a post and made to watch.
That's enough for now. Lie back. Try to relax.
No, that's not all.
They kept it up for two months.
We were taken to their outmost provinces.
It was always the same, and we were always made to watch,
The others and I. How he stood it, I don't know.
And then suddenly
There were no more floggings or humiliations,
The king's personal doctor saw to his back,
He was given decent clothing, and the collar was taken off,
And they treated us all with a special courtesy.
By the time we reached their capital city
His back was completely healed.
They had taken the cage apart—
But of course they didn't give us back our spears.
Then later that month, it was a warm afternoon in May,
The rest of us were marched out to the central square.
The crowds were there already, and the posts were set up,
To which we were tied in the old watching positions.
And he was brought out in the old way, and stripped,
And then tied flat on a big rectangular table
So that only his head could move.
Then the king made a short speech to the crowds,
To which they responded with gasps of wild excitement,
And which was then translated for the rest of us.
It was the sentence. He was to be flayed alive,
As slowly as possible, to drag out the pain.
And we were made to watch. The king's personal doctor,

The one who had tended his back,
Came forward with a tray of surgical knives.
They began at the feet.
And we were not allowed to close our eyes
Or to look away. When they were done, hours later,
The skin was turned over to one of their saddle-makers
To be tanned and stuffed and sewn. And for what?
A hideous life-sized doll, filled out with straw,
In the skin of the Roman Emperor, Valerian,
With blanks of mother-of-pearl under the eyelids,
And painted shells that had been prepared beforehand
For the fingernails and toenails,
Roughly cross-stitched on the inseam of the legs
And up the back to the center of the head,
Swung in the wind on a rope from the palace flag-pole;
And young girls were brought there by their mothers
To be told about the male anatomy.
His death had taken hours.
They were very patient.
And with him passed away the honor of Rome.

In the end, I was ransomed. Mother paid for me.
You must rest now. You must. Lean back.
Look at the flowers.
Yes. I am looking. I wish I could be like them.

PIG

In the manger of course were cows and the Child Himself
               Was like unto a lamb
Who should come in the fulness of time on an ass's back
               Into Jerusalem

And all things be redeemed—the suckling babe
               Lie safe in the serpent's home
And the lion eat straw like the ox and roar its love
               to Mark and to Jerome

And God's Peaceable Kingdom return among them all
               Save one full of offense
Into which the thousand fiends of a human soul
               Were cast and driven hence

And the one thus cured gone up into the hills
               To worship and to pray:
O Swine that takest away our sins
               That takest away

OSTIA ANTICA

for William and Dale MacDonald

Given this light,
The departing thunderhead in its anger
Off to one side, and given
These ancient stones in their setting, themselves refreshed
And rendered strangely younger
By wetness alive with the wriggling brass of heaven,
Where is the spirit's part unwashed
Of all poor spite?

The cypress thrust,
Greened in the glass of air as never
Since the first greenness offered,
Not to desire our prayer: "To ghostly creatures,
Peace, and an end of fever
Till all this dust assemble," but delivered
To their resistless lives and natures,
Rise as they must.

And the broken wall
Is only itself, deeply accepting
The sun's warmth to its bricks.
The puddles blink; a snail marches the Roman
Road of its own adopting.
The marble nymph is stripped to the flush of sex
As if in truth this timeless, human
Instant were all.

Is it the bird's
Voice, the delicious voice of water,
Addresses us on the splendid
Topic of love? And promises to youth
Still livelier forms and whiter?
Here are quick freshes, here is the body suspended
In its firm blessing, here the mouth
Finds out its words.

See, they arise
In the sign of ivy, the young males
To their strength, the meadows restored;
Concupiscence of eye, and the world's pride;
Of love, the naked skills.
At the pool's edge, the rippled image cleared,
That face set among leaves is glad,
Noble and wise.

What was begun,
The mastered force, breeds and is healing.
Pebbles and clover speak.
Each hanging waterdrop burns with a fierce
Bead of the sun's instilling.
But softly, beneath the flutesong and volatile shriek
Of birds, are to be heard discourse
Mother and son.

"If there were hushed
To us the images of earth, its poles
Hushed, and the waters of it,
And hushed the tumult of the flesh, even
The voice intrinsic of our souls,
Each tongue and token hushed and the long habit
Of thought, if that first light, the given
To us were hushed,

So that the washed
Object, fixed in the sun, were dumb,
And to the mind its brilliance
Were from beyond itself, and the mind were clear
As the unclouded dome
Wherein all things diminish, in that silence
Might we not confidently hear
God as he wished?"

Then from the grove
Suddenly falls a flight of bells.
A figure moves from the wood,
Darkly approaching at the hour of vespers
Along the ruined walls.
And bearing heavy articles of blood
And symbols of endurance, whispers,
"This is love."

THE DOVER BITCH   *A Criticism of Life*

for Andrews Wanning

So there stood Matthew Arnold and this girl
With the cliffs of England crumbling away behind them,
And he said to her, "Try to be true to me,
And I'll do the same for you, for things are bad
All over, etc., etc."
Well now, I knew this girl. It's true she had read
Sophocles in a fairly good translation
And caught that bitter allusion to the sea,
But all the time he was talking she had in mind
The notion of what his whiskers would feel like
On the back of her neck. She told me later on
That after a while she got to looking out
At the lights across the channel, and really felt sad,
Thinking of all the wine and enormous beds
And blandishments in French and the perfumes.
And then she got really angry. To have been brought
All the way down from London, and then be addressed
As a sort of mournful cosmic last resort
Is really tough on a girl, and she was pretty.
Anyway, she watched him pace the room
And finger his watch-chain and seem to sweat a bit,
And then she said one or two unprintable things.
But you mustn't judge her by that. What I mean to say is,
She's really all right. I still see her once in a while
And she always treats me right. We have a drink
And I give her a good time, and perhaps it's a year
Before I see her again, but there she is,
Running to fat, but dependable as they come.
And sometimes I bring her a bottle of *Nuit d'Amour*.

TO A MADONNA *Ex-Voto in the Spanish Style*

for Allen Tate

Madonna, mistress, I shall build for you
An altar of my misery, and hew
Out of my heart's remote and midnight pitch,
Far from all worldly lusts and sneers, a niche
Enamelled totally in gold and blue
Where I shall set you up and worship you.
And of my verse, like hammered silver lace
Studded with amethysts of rhyme, I'll place
A hand-wrought crown upon your head, and I'll
Make you a coat in the barbaric style,
Picked out in seedling tears instead of pearl,
That you shall wear like mail, my mortal girl,
Lined with suspicion, made of jealousy,
Encasing all your charms, that none may see.
As for the intimate part of your attire,
Your dress shall be composed of my desire,
Rising and falling, swirling from your knees
To your round hills and deep declivities.
Of the respect I owe you I shall make
A pair of satin shoes that they may take—
Though most unworthily prepared to do it—
The authentic shape and imprint of your foot.
And if I fail, for all my proffered boon,
To make a silver footstool of the moon,
Victorious queen, I place beneath your heel
The head of this black serpent that I feel
Gnawing at my intestines all the time,
Swollen with hate and venomous with crime.
You shall behold my thoughts like tapers lit
Before your flowered shrine, and brightening it,
Reflected in the semi-dome's clear skies
Like so many fierce stars or fiery eyes.
And I shall be as myrrh and frankincense,
Rising forever in a smoky trance,
And the dark cloud of my tormented hopes

Shall lift in yearning toward your snowy slopes.
And finally, to render you more real,
I shall make seven blades of Spanish steel
Out of the Seven Deadly Sins, and I
Shall mix my love with murderous savagery,
And like a circus knife-thrower, I'll aim
At the pure center of your gentle frame,
And plunge those blades into your beating heart,
Your bleeding, suffering, palpitating heart.

(AFTER BAUDELAIRE)

CLAIR DE LUNE

Powder and scent and silence. The young dwarf
Shoulders his lute. The moon is Levantine.
It settles its pearl in every glass of wine.
Harlequin is already at the wharf.

The gallant is masked. A pressure of his thumb
Communicates cutaneous interest.
On the smooth upward swelling of a breast
A small black heart is fixed with spirit gum.

The thieving moment is now. Deftly, Pierrot
Exits, bearing a tray of fruits and coins.
A monkey, chained by his tiny loins,
Is taken aboard. They let their moorings go.

Silence. Even the god shall soon be gone.
Shadows, in their cool, tidal enterprise,
Have eaten away his muscular stone thighs.
Moonlight edges across the empty lawn.

Taffeta whispers. Someone is staring through
The white ribs of the pergola. She stares
At a small garnet pulse that disappears
Steadily seaward. Ah, my dear, it is you.

But you are not alone. A gardener goes
Through the bone light about the dark estate.
He bows, and, cheerfully inebriate,
Admires the lunar ashes of a rose,

And sings to his imaginary loves.
Wait. You can hear him. The familiar notes
Drift toward the old moss-bottomed fishing boats:
"Happy the heart that thinks of no removes."

This is your nightmare. Those cold hands are yours.
The pain in the drunken singing is your pain.
Morning will taste of bitterness again.
The heart turns to a stone, but it endures.

THREE PROMPTERS FROM THE WINGS

for George and Mary Dimock

ATROPOS: OR, THE FUTURE

He rushed out of the temple
And for all his young good looks,
Excellence at wrestling,
High and manly pride,
The giddy world's own darling,
He thought of suicide.
(The facts are clear and simple
But are not found in books.)

Think how the young suppose
That any minute now
Some darkly beautiful
Stranger's leg or throat
Will speak out in the taut
Inflections of desire,
Will choose them, will allow
Each finger its own thought
And whatever it reaches for.
A vision without clothes
Tickles the genitalia
And makes blithe the heart.
But in this most of all
He was cut out for failure.

That morning smelled of hay.
But all that he found tempting
Was a high, weathered cliff.
Now at a subtle prompting
He hesitated. If
He ended down below
He had overcome the Fates;
The oracle was false;
The gods themselves were blind.

A fate he could contravene
Was certainly not Fate.
All lay in his power.
(How this came to his mind
No child of man can say.
The clear, rational light
Touches on less than half,
And "he who hesitates . . ."
For who could presume to know
The decisive, inward pulse
Of things?)
   After an hour
He rose to his full height,
The master of himself.

That morning smelled of hay,
The day was clear. A moisture
Cooled at the tips of leaves.
The fields were overlaid
With light. It was harvest time.
Three swallows appraised the day,
And bearing aloft their lives,
Sailed into a wild climb,
Then spilled across the pasture
Like water over tiles.
One could have seen for miles
The sun on a knife-blade.
And there he stood, the hero,
With a lascivious wind
Sliding across his chest,
(The sort of thing that women,
Who are fools the whole world over,
Would fondle and adore
And stand before undressed.)
But deep within his loins
A bitterness is set.
He is already blind.

The faceless powers summon
To their eternal sorrow
The handsome, bold, and vain,
And those dark things are met
At a place where three roads join.
They touch with an open sore
The lips that he shall kiss.
And some day men may call me,
Because I'm old and plain
And never had a lover,
The authoress of this.

CLOTHO: OR, THE PRESENT

Well, there he stands, surrounded
By all his kith and kin,
Townspeople and friends,
As the evidence rolls in,
And don't go telling me
The spectacle isn't silly.

A prince in low disguise,
Moving among the humble
With kingly purposes
Is an old, romantic posture,
And always popular.
He started on this career
By overthrowing Fate
(A splendid accomplishment,
And all done in an hour)
That crucial day at the temple
When the birds crossed over the pasture
As was said by my sister, here.
Which goes to show that an omen
Is a mere tissue of lies

To please the superstitious
And keep the masses content.
From this initial success
He moved on without pause
To outwit and subdue a vicious
Beast with lion's paws,
The wings of a great bird,
And the breasts and face of a woman.
This meant knowing no less
Than the universal state
Of man. Which is quite a lot.
(Construe this as you please.)

Now today an old abuse
Raises its head and festers
To the scandal and disease
Of all. He will weed it out
And cleanse the earth of it.
Clearly, if anyone could,
He can redeem these lands;
To doubt this would be absurd.
The finest faculties,
Courage and will and wit
He has patiently put to use
For Truth and the Common Good,
And lordly above the taunts
Of his enemies, there he stands,
The father of his sisters,
His daughters their own aunts.

Some sentimental fool
Invented the Tragic Muse.
She doesn't exist at all.
For human life is composed
In reasonably equal parts
Of triumph and chagrin,
And the parts are so hotly fused

As to seem a single thing.
This is true as well
Of wisdom and ignorance
And of happiness and pain:
Nothing is purely itself
But is linked with its antidote
In cold self-mockery—
A fact with which only those
Born with a Comic sense
Can learn to content themselves.
While heroes die to maintain
Some part of existence clean
And incontaminate.

Now take this fellow here
Who is about to find
The summit of his life
Founded upon disaster.
Lovers can learn as much
Every night in bed,
For whatever flesh can touch
Is never quite enough.
They know it is tempting fate
To hold out for perfect bliss.
And yet the whole world over
Blind men will choose as master
To lead them the most blind.
And some day men may call me,
Because I'm old and tough,
And never had a lover,
The instrument of this.

LACHESIS: OR, THE PAST

Well, now. You might suppose
There's nothing left to be said.

Outcast, corrupt and blind,
He knows it's night when an owl
Wakes up to hoot at the wise,
And the owl inside his head
Looks out of sightless eyes,
Answers, and sinks its toes
Into the soft and bloody
Center of his mind.

But miles and miles away
Suffers another man.
He was young, open-hearted,
Strong in mind and body
When all these things began.
Every blessed night
He attends the moonstruck owl,
Familiar of the witless,
And remembers a dark day,
A new-born baby's howl,
And an autumnal wetness.

The smallest sign of love
Is always an easy target
For the jealous and cynical.
Perhaps, indeed, they are right.
I leave it for you to say.
But to leave a little child,
Roped around the feet,
To the charities of a wolf
Was more than he could stomach.
He weighed this for an hour,
Then rose to his full height,
The master of himself.
And the last, clinching witness.
The great life he spared
He would return to punish
And punish himself as well.

But recently his woes
Are muted by the moon.
He no longer goes alone.
Thorns have befriended him,
And once he found his mother
Hiding under a stone.
She was fat, wet, and lame.
She said it was clever of him
To find her in the dark
But he always had been a wise one,
And warned him against snails.
And now his every word
Is free of all human hates
And human kindliness.
To be mad, as the world goes,
Is not the worst of fates.
(And please do not forget
There are those who find this comic.)

But what, you ask, of the hero?
(Ah well, I am very old
And they say I have a rambling
Or a devious sort of mind.)
At midnight and in rain
He advances without trembling
From sorrow unto sorrow
Toward a kind of light
The sun makes upon metal
Which perhaps even the blind
May secretly behold.
What the intelligence
Works out in pure delight
The body must learn in pain.
He has solved the Sphinx's riddle
In his own ligaments.

And now in a green place,
Holy and unknown,
He has taken off his clothes.
Dust in the sliding light
Swims and is gone. Fruit
Thickens. The listless cello
Of flies tuning in shadows
Wet bark and the silver click
Of water over stones
Are close about him where
He stands, an only witness
With no eyes in his face.
In spite of which he knows
Clear as he once had known,
Though bound both hand and foot,
The smell of mountain air
And an autumnal wetness.
And he sees, moreover,
Unfolding into the light
Three pairs of wings in flight,
Moving as water moves.
The strength, wisdom and bliss
Of their inhuman loves
They scatter near the temple.
And some day men may call me,
Because I'm old and simple
And never had a lover,
Responsible for this.

LIZARDS AND SNAKES

On the summer road that ran by our front porch
        Lizards and snakes came out to sun.
It was hot as a stove out there, enough to scorch
        A buzzard's foot. Still, it was fun
To lie in the dust and spy on them. Near but remote,
        They snoozed in the carriage ruts, a smile
In the set of the jaw, a fierce pulse in the throat
Working away like Jack Doyle's after he'd run the mile.

Aunt Martha had an unfair prejudice
        Against them (as well as being cold
Toward bats.) She was pretty inflexible in this,
        Being a spinster and all, and old.
So we used to slip them into her knitting box.
        In the evening she'd bring in things to mend
And a nice surprise would slide out from under the socks.
It broadened her life, as Joe said. Joe was my friend.

But we never did it again after the day
        Of the big wind when you could hear the trees
Creak like rockingchairs. She was looking away
        Off, and kept saying, "Sweet Jesus, please
Don't let him near me. He's as like as twins.
        He can crack us like lice with his fingernail.
I can see him plain as a pikestaff. Look how he grins
And swinges the scaly horror of his folded tail."

ADAM

Hath the rain a father? or who hath begotten the drops of dew?

"Adam, my child, my son,
These very words you hear
Compose the fish and starlight
Of your untroubled dream.
When you awake, my child,
It shall all come true.
Know that it was for you
That all things were begun."

Adam, my child, my son,
Thus spoke Our Father in heaven
To his first, fabled child,
The father of us all.
And I, your father, tell
The words over again
As innumerable men
From ancient times have done.

Tell them again in pain,
And to the empty air.
Where you are men speak
A different mother tongue.
Will you forget our games,
Our hide-and-seek and song?
Child, it will be long
Before I see you again.

Adam, there will be
Many hard hours,
As an old poem says,
Hours of loneliness.
I cannot ease them for you;
They are our common lot.
During them, like as not,
You will dream of me.

When you are crouched away
In a strange clothes closet
Hiding from one who's "It"
And the dark crowds in,
Do not be afraid—
O, if you can, believe
In a father's love
That you shall know some day.

Think of the summer rain
Or seedpearls of the mist;
Seeing the beaded leaf,
Try to remember me.
From far away
I send my blessing out
To circle the great globe.
It shall reach you yet.

THE ORIGIN OF CENTAURS

for Dimitri Hadzi

But to the girdle do the gods inherit,
Beneath is all the fiend's.   KING LEAR

This mild September mist recalls the soul
        To its own lust;
     On the enchanted lawn
It sees the iron top of the flagpole
     Sublimed away and gone
Into Parnassian regions beyond rust;
And would undo the body to less than dust.

Sundial and juniper have been dispelled
        Into thin air.
     The pale ghost of a leaf
Haunts those uncanny softnesses that felled
     And whitely brought to grief
The trees that only yesterday were there.
The soul recoils into its old despair,

Knowing that though the horizon is at hand,
        Twelve paltry feet
     Refuse to be traversed,
And form themselves before wherever you stand
     As if you were accursed;
While stones drift from the field, and the arbor-seat
Floats toward some *millefleurs* world of summer heat.

Yet from the void where the azalea bush
        Departed hence,
     Sadly the soul must hear
Twitter and cricket where should be all hush,
     And from the belvedere
A muffled grunt survives in evidence
That love must sweat under the weight of sense.

Or so once thought a man in a Greek mist—
      Who set aside
    The wine-cup and the wine,
And that deep fissure he alone had kissed,
    All circumscribing line,
Moved to the very edge in one swift stride
And took those shawls of nothing for his bride.

Was it the Goddess herself? Some dense embrace
      Closed like a bath
    Of love about his head;
Perfectly silent and without a face.
    Blindfolded on her bed,
He could see nothing but the aftermath:
Those powerful, clear hoofprints on the path.

THE VOW

In the third month, a sudden flow of blood.
The mirth of tabrets ceaseth, and the joy
Also of the harp. The frail image of God
Lay spilled and formless. Neither girl nor boy,
But yet blood of my blood, nearly my child.
     All that long day
Her pale face turned to the window's mild
     Featureless grey.

And for some nights she whimpered as she dreamed
The dead thing spoke, saying: "Do not recall
Pleasure at my conception. I am redeemed
From pain and sorrow. Mourn rather for all
Who breathlessly issue from the bone gates,
     The gates of horn,
For truly it is best of all the fates
     Not to be born.

"Mother, a child lay gasping for bare breath
On Christmas Eve when Santa Claus had set
Death in the stocking, and the lights of death
Flamed in the tree. O, if you can, forget
You were the child, turn to my father's lips
     Against the time
When his cold hand puts forth its fingertips
     Of jointed lime."

Doctors of Science, what is man that he
Should hope to come to a good end? *The best
Is not to have been born.* And could it be
That Jewish diligence and Irish jest
The consent of flesh and a midwinter storm
     Had reconciled,
Was yet too bold a mixture to inform
     A simple child?

Even as gold is tried, Gentile and Jew.
If that ghost was a girl's, I swear to it:
Your mother shall be far more blessed than you.
And if a boy's, I swear: The flames are lit
That shall refine us; they shall not destroy
       A living hair.
Your younger brothers shall confirm in joy
       This that I swear.

HEUREUX QUI, COMME ULYSSE,
A FAIT UN BEAU VOYAGE...

for Claire White

Great joy be to the sailor if he chart
The Odyssey or bear away the Fleece
Yet unto wisdom's laurel and the peace
Of his own kind come lastly to his start.
And when shall I, being migrant, bring my heart
Home to its plots of parsley, its proper earth,
Pot hooks, cow dung, black chimney bricks whose worth
I have not skill to honor in my art.

My home, my father's and grandfather's home.
Not the imperial porphyry of Rome
But slate is my true stone, slate is my blue.
And bluer the Loire is to my reckoning
Than Caesar's Tiber, and more nourishing
Than salt spray is the breathing of Anjou.

(AFTER DU BELLAY)

RITES AND CEREMONIES

I THE ROOM

Father, adonoi, author of all things,
            of the three states,
the soft light on the barn at dawn,
            a wind that sings
in the bracken, fire in iron grates,
            the ram's horn,
Furnisher, hinger of heaven, who bound
            the lovely Pleaides,
entered the perfect treasuries of the snow,
            established the round
course of the world, birth, death and disease
            and caused to grow
veins, brain, bones in me, to breathe and sing
            fashioned me air,
Lord, who, governing cloud and waterspout,
            o my King,
held me alive till this my forty-third year—
            in whom we doubt—
Who was that child of whom they tell
            in lauds and threnes?
whose holy name all shall pronounce
            Emmanuel,
which being interpreted means,
            "Gott mit uns"?

I saw it on their belts. A young one, dead,
Left there on purpose to get us used to the sight
When we first moved in. Helmet spilled off, head
Blond and boyish and bloody. I was scared that night.
And the sign was there,
The sign of the child, the grave, worship and loss,
Gunpowder heavy as pollen in winter air,
An Iron Cross.

38

It is twenty years now, Father. I have come home.
But in the camps, one can look through a huge square
Window, like an aquarium, upon a room
The size of my livingroom filled with human hair.
Others have shoes, or valises
Made mostly of cardboard, which once contained
Pills, fresh diapers. This is one of the places
Never explained.

Out of one trainload, about five hundred in all,
Twenty the next morning were hopelessly insane.
And some there be that have no memorial,
That are perished as though they had never been.
Made into soap.
Who now remembers "The Singing Horses of Buchenwald"?
"Above all, the saving of lives," whispered the Pope.
Die Vögelein schweigen im Walde,

But for years the screaming continued, night and day,
And the little children were suffered to come along, too.
At night, Father, in the dark, when I pray,
I am there, I am there. I am pushed through
With the others to the strange room
Without windows; whitewashed walls, cement floor.
Millions, Father, millions have come to this pass,
Which a great church has voted to "deplore."

Are the vents in the ceiling, Father, to let the spirit depart?
We are crowded in here naked, female and male.
An old man is saying a prayer. And now we start
To panic, to claw at each other, to wail
As the rubber-edged door closes on chance and choice.
He is saying a prayer for all whom this room shall kill.
"I cried unto the Lord God with my voice,
And He has heard me out His holy hill."

II   THE FIRE SERMON

Small paw tracks in the snow, eloquent of a passage
Neither seen nor heard. Over the timbered hill,
Turning at the fence, and under the crisp light of winter,
In blue shadows, trailing toward the town.
Beginning at the outposts, the foxtrot of death,
Silent and visible, slipped westward from the holy original
      east.
Even in "our sea" on a misty Easter
Ships were discovered adrift, heavy with pepper and tea,
The whole crew dead.

          Was it a judgment?

Among the heathen, the king of Tharsis, seeing
Such sudden slaughter of his people, began a journey to
      Avignon
With a great multitude of his nobles, to propose to the pope
That he become a Christian and be baptized,
Thinking that he might assuage the anger of God
Upon his people for their wicked unbelief.
But when he had journeyed twenty days,
He heard the pestilence had struck among the Christians
As among other peoples. So, turning in his tracks,
He travelled no farther, but hastened to return home.
The Christians, pursuing these people from behind,
Slew about seven thousand of them.

At the horse-trough, at dusk,
In the morning among the fishbaskets,
The soft print of the dancing-master's foot.

In Marseilles, one hundred and fifty Friars Minor.
In the region of Provence, three hundred and fifty-eight
Of the Friars Preachers died in Lent.

If it was a judgment, it struck home in the houses of
    penitence,
The meek and the faithful were in no wise spared.
Prayer and smoke were thought a protection.
Braziers smoldered all day on the papal floors.

During this same year, there was a great mortality
Of sheep everywhere in the kingdom;
In one place and in one pasture, more than five thousand
    sheep
Died and became so putrified
That neither beast nor bird wanted to touch them.
And the price of everything was cheap,
Because of the fear of death.

How could it be a judgment,
The children in convulsions, the sweating and stink,
And not enough living to bury the dead?
The shepherd had abandoned his sheep.

And presently it was found to be
Not a judgment.

The old town council had first to be deposed
And a new one elected, whose views agreed
With the will of the people. And a platform erected,
Not very high, perhaps only two inches above the tallest
    headstone,
But easy to view. And underneath it, concealed,
The excess lumber and nails, some logs, old brooms and
    straw,
Piled on the ancient graves. The preparations were hasty
But thorough, they were thorough.
A visitor to that town today is directed to
The Minster. The Facade, by Erwin von Steinbach,
Is justly the most admired part of the edifice
And presents a singularly happy union

Of the style of Northern France
With the perpendicular tendency
Peculiar to German cathedrals.
No signs of the platform are left, which in any case
Was outside the town walls.
But on that day, Saturday, February 14th,
The Sabbath, and dedicated to St. Valentine,
Everyone who was not too sick was down
To watch the ceremony. The clergy,
The new town council, the students
Of the university which later gave Goethe
His degree of Doctor of Laws.
For the evidence now was in: in Berne, under torture,
Two Jews had confessed to poisoning the wells.
Wherefore throughout Europe were these platforms erected,
Even as here in the city of Strasbourg,
And the Jews assembled upon them,
Children and all, and tied together with rope.

It is barren hereabout
And the wind is cold,
And the sound of prayer, clamor of curse and shout
Is blown past the sheepfold
Out of hearing.

The river worms through the snow plain
In kindless darks.
And man is born to sorrow and to pain
As surely as the sparks
Fly upward.

Father, among these many souls
Is there not one
Whom thou shalt pluck for love out of the coals?
Look, look, they have begun
To douse the rags.

O that thou shouldst give dust a tongue
To crie to thee,
And then not heare it crying! Who is strong
When the flame eats his knee?
O hear my prayer,

And let my cry come unto thee.
Hide not thy face.
Let there some child among us worthy be
Here to receive thy grace
And sheltering.

It is barren hereabout
And the wind is cold,
And the crack of fire, melting of prayer and shout
Is blown past the sheepfold
Out of hearing.

III   THE DREAM

The contemplation of horror is not edifying,
Neither does it strengthen the soul.
And the gentle serenity in the paintings of martyrs,
St. Lucy, bearing her eyes on a plate,
St. Cecilia, whose pipes were the pipes of plumbing
And whose music was live steam,
The gridiron tilting lightly against the sleeve of
St. Lawrence,
These, and others, bewilder and shame us.
Not all among us are of their kind.
Fear of our own imperfections,
Fear learned and inherited,
Fear shapes itself in dreams
Not more fantastic than the brute fact.

43

It is the first Saturday in Carnival.
There, in the Corso, homesick Du Bellay.
Yesterday it was acrobats, and a play
About Venetian magnificos, and in the interval
Bull-baiting, palm-reading, juggling, but today

The race. Observe how sad he appears to be:
Thinking perhaps of Anjou, the climbing grace
Of smoke from a neighbor's chimney, of a place
Slate-roofed and kindly. The vast majesty
Of Rome is lost on him. But not the embrace

Of the lovers. See, see young harlequins bent
On stealing kisses from their columbines.
Here are the *dolces*, here the inebriate wines
Before the seemly austerities of Lent.
The couples form tight-packed, irregular lines

On each side of the mile-long, gorgeous course.
The men have whips and sticks with bunting tied
About them. Anointed Folly and his bride
Ordain Misrule. Camel and Barbary horse
Shall feel the general mirth upon their hide.

First down the gantlet, twenty chosen asses,
Grey, Midas-eared, mild beasts receive the jeers
And clouts of the young crowd. Consort of brasses
Salutes the victor at the far end. Glasses
Are filled again, the men caress their dears,

The children shout. But who are these that stand
And shuffle shyly at the starting line?
Twenty young men, naked, except the band
Around their loins, wait for the horn's command.
Christ's Vicar chose them, and imposed his fine.

Du Bellay, poet, take no thought of them;
And yet they too are exiles, and have said
Through many generations, long since dead,
"*If I forget thee, O Jerusalem, . . .*"
Still, others have been scourged and buffeted

And worse. Think rather, if you must,
Of Piranesian, elegaic woes,
Rome's grand declensions, that all-but-speaking dust.
Or think of the young gallants and their lust.
Or wait for the next heat, the buffaloes.

IV   WORDS FOR THE DAY OF ATONEMENT

Merely to have survived is not an index of excellence,
Nor, given the way things go,
Even of low cunning.
Yet I have seen the wicked in great power,
And spreading himself like a green bay tree.
And the good as if they had never been;
Their voices are blown away on the winter wind.
And again we wander the wilderness
For our transgressions
Which are confessed in the daily papers.

Except the Lord of hosts had left unto us
A very small remnant,
We should have been as Sodom,
We should have been like unto Gomorrah.
And to what purpose, as the darkness closes about
And the child screams in the jellied fire,
Had best be our present concern,
Here, in this wilderness of comfort
In which we dwell.
                    Shall we now consider
The suspicious postures of our virtue,

The deformed consequences of our love,
The painful issues of our mildest acts?
Shall we ask,
Where is there one
Mad, poor and betrayed enough to find
Forgiveness for us, saying,
"None does offend,
None, I say,
None"?

Listen, listen.
But the voices are blown away.

And yet, this light,
The work of thy fingers, . . .

The soul is thine, and the body is thy creation:
O have compassion on thy handiwork.
The soul is thine, and the body is thine:
O deal with us according to thy name.
We come before thee relying on thy name;
O deal with us according to thy name;
For the sake of the glory of thy name;
As the gracious and merciful God is thy name.
O Lord, for thy name's sake we plead,
Forgive us our sins, though they be very great.

It is winter as I write.
For miles the holy treasuries of snow
Sag the still world with white,
And all soft shapes are washed from top to toe
In pigeon-colored light.

Tree, bush and weed maintain
Their humbled, lovely postures all day through.
And darkly in the brain
The famous ancient questions gather: Who
Fathered the fathering rain

That falleth in the wilderness
Where no man is, wherein there is no man;
    To satisfy the cress,
Knotweed and moonwort? And shall scan
    Our old unlawfulness?

Who shall profess to understand
The diligence and purpose of the rose?
    Yet deep as to some gland,
A promised odor, even among these snows,
    Steals in like contraband.

Forgiven be the whole Congregation of the Children of Israel,
and the stranger dwelling in their midst. For all the people
have inadvertently sinned.

    Father, I also pray
For those among us whom we know not, those
    Dearest to thy grace,
The saved and saving remnant, the promised third,
    Who in a later day
When we again are compassed about with foes,
Shall be for us a nail in thy holy place
There to abide according to thy word.

    Neither shall the flame
Kindle upon them, nor the fire burn
    A hair of them, for they
Shall be thy care when it shall come to pass,
    And calling on thy name
In the hot kilns and ovens, they shall turn
To thee as it is prophesied, and say,
"He shall come down like rain upon mown grass."

A LETTER

I have been wondering
What you are thinking about, and by now suppose
It is certainly not me.
But the crocus is up, and the lark, and the blundering
Blood knows what it knows.
It talks to itself all night, like a sliding moonlit sea.

Of course, it is talking of you.
At dawn, where the ocean has netted its catch of lights,
The sun plants one lithe foot
On that spill of mirrors, but the blood goes worming
through
Its warm Arabian nights,
Naming your pounding name again in the dark heart-root.

Who shall, of course, be nameless.
Anyway, I should want you to know I have done my
best,
As I'm sure you have, too.
Others are bound to us, the gentle and blameless
Whose names are not confessed
In the ceaseless palaver. My dearest, the clear unquarried blue

Of those depths is all but blinding.
You may remember that once you brought my boys
Two little woolly birds.
Yesterday the older one asked for you upon finding
Your thrush among his toys.
And the tides welled about me, and I could find no words.

There is not much else to tell.
One tries one's best to continue as before,
Doing some little good.
But I would have you know that all is not well
With a man dead set to ignore
The endless repetitions of his own murmurous blood.

THE SEVEN DEADLY SINS

Wood engravings by Leonard Baskin

PRIDE

"For me Almighty God Himself has died,"
Said one who formerly rebuked his pride
With, "Father, I am not worthy," and here denied
The Mercy by which each of us is tried.

E N V Y

When, to a popular tune, God's Mercy and Justice
      Coagulate here again,
Establishing in tissue the True Republic
      Of good looks to all men
And victuals and wit and the holy sloth of the lily,
      Thou shalt not toil nor spin.

WRATH

I saw in stalls of pearl the heavenly hosts,
Gentle as down, and without private parts.
"Dies Irae," they sang, and I could smell
The dead-white phosphorus of sacred hearts.

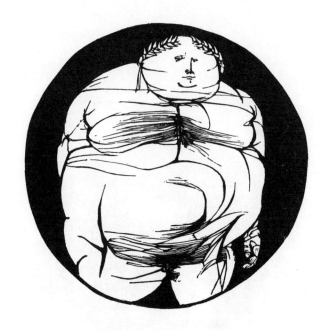

SLOTH

The first man leaps the ditch. (Who wins this race
      Wins laurel, but laurel dies.)
The next falls in (who in his hour of grace
      Plucked out his offending eyes.)
The blind still lead. (Consider the ant's ways;
      Consider, and be wise.)

AVARICE

The penniless Indian fakirs and their camels
    Slip through the needle's eye
To bliss (for neither flesh nor spirit trammels
    Such as are prone to die)
And from emaciate heaven they behold
    Our sinful kings confer
Upon an infant huge tributes of gold
    And frankincense and myrrh.

GLUTTONY

Let the poor look to themselves, for it is said
Their savior wouldn't turn stones into bread.
And let the sow continually say grace.
For moss shall build in the lung and leave no trace,
The glutton worm shall tunnel in the head
And eat the Word out of the parchment face.

LUST

The Phoenix knows no lust, and Christ, our mother,
Suckles his children with his vintage blood.
Not to be such a One is to be other.

UPON THE DEATH OF
GEORGE SANTAYANA

Down every passage of the cloister hung
A dark wood cross on a white plaster wall;
But in the court were roses, not as tongue
Might have them, something of Christ's blood grown small,
But just as roses, and at three o'clock
Their essences, inseparably bouqueted,
Seemed more than Christ's last breath, and rose to mock
An elderly man for whom the Sisters prayed.

What heart can know itself? The Sibyl speaks
Mirthless and unbedizened things, but who
Can fathom her intent? Loving the Greeks,
He whispered to a nun who strove to woo
His spirit unto God by prayer and fast,
"Pray that I go to Limbo, if it please
Heaven to let my soul regard at last
Democritus, Plato and Socrates."

And so it was. The river, as foretold,
Ran darkly by; under his tongue he found
Coin for the passage; the ferry tossed and rolled;
The sages stood on their appointed ground,
Sighing, all as foretold. The mind was tasked;
He had not dreamed that so many had died.
"But where is Alcibiades," he asked,
"The golden roisterer, the animal pride?"

Those sages who had spoken of the love
And enmity of things, how all things flow,
Stood in a light no life is witness of,
And Socrates, whose wisdom was to know
He did not know, spoke with a solemn mien,
And all his wonderful ugliness was lit,
"He whom I loved for what he might have been
Freezes with traitors in the ultimate pit."

BIRDWATCHERS OF AMERICA

I suffer now continually from ver-
tigo, and today, 23rd of January,
1862, I received a singular warning:
I felt the wind of the wing of mad-
ness pass over me.

BAUDELAIRE, *Journals*

It's all very well to dream of a dove that saves,
    Picasso's or the Pope's,
The one that annually coos in Our Lady's ear
    Half the world's hopes,
And the other one that shall cunningly engineer
The retirement of all businessmen to their graves,
    And when this is brought about
Make us the loving brothers of every lout—

But in our part of the country a false dusk
    Lingers for hours; it steams
From the soaked hay, wades in the cloudy woods,
    Engendering other dreams.
Formless and soft beyond the fence it broods
Or rises as a faint and rotten musk
    Out of a broken stalk.
There are some things of which we seldom talk;

For instance, the woman next door, whom we hear at night,
    Claims that when she was small
She found a man stone dead near the cedar trees
    After the first snowfall.
The air was clear. He seemed in ultimate peace
Except that he had no eyes. Rigid and bright
    Upon the forehead, furred
With a light frost, crouched an outrageous bird.

THE SONG OF THE FLEA

Beware of those that flatter;
Likewise beware of those
That would redress the matter
By publishing their woes.
They would corrupt your nature
For their own purposes
And taint God's every creature
With pestilent disease.

Now look you in the mirror
And swear to your own face
It never dealt in error
With pity or with praise.
Swear that there is no Circe,
And swear me, if you can,
That without aid or mercy
You are but your own man.

If you can swear thus nimbly
Then we can end our wars
And join in the assembly
Of jungle predators,
For honestly to thieve
Bespeaks a brotherhood:
Without a "by your leave"
I live upon your blood.

THE MAN WHO MARRIED MAGDALENE

Variation on a Theme by Louis Simpson

> *Then said the Lord, dost thou well to be angry?*

I have been in this bar
For close to seven days.
The dark girl over there,
For a modest dollar, lays.

And you can get a blow-job
Where other men have pissed
In the little room that's sacred
To the Evangelist—

If you're inclined that way.
For myself, I drink and sleep.
The floor is knotty cedar
But the beer is flat and cheap.

And you can bet your life
I'll be here another seven.
Stranger, here's to my wife,
Who died and went to heaven.

She was a famous beauty,
But *our very breath is loaned.*
The rabbi's voice was fruity,
And since then I've been stoned—

A royal, nonstop bender.
But your money's no good here;
Put it away. Bartender,
Give my friend a beer.

I dreamed the other night
When the sky was full of stars
That I stood outside a gate
And looked in through the bars.

Two angels stood together.
A purple light was shed
From their every metal feather.
And then one of them said,

"It was pretty much the same
For years and years and years,
But since the Christians came
The place is full of queers.

Still, let them have their due.
Things here are far less solemn.
Instead of each beardy Jew
Muttering, 'Shalom, Shalom,'

There's a down-to-earth, informal
Fleshiness to the scene;
It's healthier, more normal,
If you know what I mean.

Such as once went to Gehenna
Now dance among the blessed.
But Mary Magdalena,
She had it the best."

And he nudged his feathered friend
And gave him a wicked leer,
And I woke up and fought back
The nausea with a beer.

What man shall understand
The Lord's mysterious way?
My tongue is thick with worship
And whiskey, and some day

I will come to in Bellevue
And make psalms unto the Lord.
But verily I tell you,
She hath her reward.

IMPROVISATIONS ON AESOP

1 It was a tortoise aspiring to fly
   That murdered Aeschylus. All men must die.

2 The crocodile rends man and beast to death
   And has St. Francis' birds to pick his teeth.

3 Lorenzo sponsored artists, and the ant
   Must save to give the grasshopper a grant.

4 The blind man bears the lame, who gives him eyes;
   Only the weak make common enterprise.

5 Frogs into bulls, sows' ears into silk purses,
   These are our hopes in youth, in age our curses.

6 Spare not the rod, lest thy child be undone,
   And at the gallows cry, "Behold thy son."

7 The Fox and Buddha put away their lust:
   "Sour grapes!" they cry, "All but the soul is dust!"

8 An ass may look at an angel, Balaam was shown;
   Cudgel thy wits, and leave thine ass alone.

9 Is not that pastoral instruction sweet
   Which says who shall be eaten, who shall eat?

THE THOUGHTFUL ROISTERER
DECLINES THE GAMBIT

I'm not going to get myself shot full of holes
For comparative strangers, like Richelieu or the King;
I prefer to investigate how a coward may cling
To the modest ways of simple civilian souls.
If I couldn't put down a little bit of the hair
Of the dog each day, I'd be as good as dead;
And it's nothing to me that a man will die in bed
Or under the table without the *Croix de Guerre.*

So as far as I'm concerned, you can drop the act
About the Immortal Fame and Illustrious End.
I shall die unsung, but with all of me intact,
Toasting His Noble Majesty and His Grace.
And if I die by the mouth, believe me, friend,
It won't be the cannon's mouth, in any case.

(AFTER CHARLES VION DE DALIBRAY)

GIANT TORTOISE

I am related to stones
The slow accretion of moss where dirt is wedged
Long waxy hair that can split boulders.
Events are not important.

I live in my bone
Recalling the hour of my death.
It takes more toughness than most have got.
Or a saintliness.

Strength of a certain kind, anyway.
Bald toothless clumsy perhaps
With all the indignity of old age
But age is not important.

There is nothing worth remembering
But the silver glint in the muck
The thickening of great trees
The hard crust getting harder.

"MORE LIGHT! MORE LIGHT!"

for Heinrich Blücher and Hannah Arendt

Composed in the Tower before his execution
These moving verses, and being brought at that time
Painfully to the stake, submitted, declaring thus:
"I implore my God to witness that I have made no crime."

Nor was he forsaken of courage, but the death was horrible,
The sack of gunpowder failing to ignite.
His legs were blistered sticks on which the black sap
Bubbled and burst as he howled for the Kindly Light.

And that was but one, and by no means one of the worst;
Permitted at least his pitiful dignity;
And such as were by made prayers in the name of Christ,
That shall judge all men, for his soul's tranquillity.

We move now to outside a German wood.
Three men are there commanded to dig a hole
In which the two Jews are ordered to lie down
And be buried alive by the third, who is a Pole.

Not light from the shrine at Weimar beyond the hill
Nor light from heaven appeared. But he did refuse.
A Lüger settled back deeply in its glove.
He was ordered to change places with the Jews.

Much casual death had drained away their souls.
The thick dirt mounted toward the quivering chin.
When only the head was exposed the order came
To dig him out again and to get back in.

No light, no light in the blue Polish eye.
When he finished a riding boot packed down the earth.
The Lüger hovered lightly in its glove.
He was shot in the belly and in three hours bled to death.

No prayers or incense rose up in those hours
Which grew to be years, and every day came mute
Ghosts from the ovens, sifting through crisp air,
And settled upon his eyes in a black soot.

"AND CAN YE SING BALULOO
WHEN THE BAIRN GREETS?"

All these years I have known of her despair.
"I was about to be happy when the abyss
  Opened its mouth. It was empty, except for this
  Yellowish sperm of horror that glistened there.

I tried so hard not to look as the thing grew fat
And pulsed in its bed of hair. I tried to think
Of Sister Marie Gerald, of our swaddled link
To the Lord of Hosts, the manger, and all of that.

None of it worked. And even the whip-lash wind,
To which I clung and begged to be blown away,
Didn't work. These eyes, that many have praised as gay,
Are the stale jellies of lust in which Adam sinned.

And nothing works. Sickened since God knows when,
Since early childhood when I first saw the horror,
I have spent hours alone before my mirror.
There is no cure for me in the world of men."

"IT OUT-HERODS HEROD.
PRAY YOU, AVOID IT."

Tonight my children hunch
Toward their Western, and are glad
As, with a Sunday punch,
The Good casts out the Bad.

And in their fairy tales
The warty giant and witch
Get sealed in doorless jails
And the match-girl strikes it rich.

I've made myself a drink.
The giant and witch are set
To bust out of the clink
When my children have gone to bed.

All frequencies are loud
With signals of despair;
In flash and morse they crowd
The rondure of the air.

For the wicked have grown strong,
Their numbers mock at death,
Their cow brings forth its young,
Their bull engendereth.

Their very fund of strength,
Satan, bestrides the globe;
He stalks its breadth and length
And finds out even Job.

Yet by quite other laws
My children make their case;
Half God, half Santa Claus,
But with my voice and face,

"It Out-Herods Herod. Pray you, avoid it."

> A hero comes to save
> The poorman, beggarman, thief,
> And make the world behave
> And put an end to grief.
>
> And that their sleep be sound
> I say this childermas
> Who could not, at one time,
> Have saved them from the gas.

FROM

A SUMMONING OF STONES

(1954)

DOUBLE SONNET

I recall everything, but more than all,
Words being nothing now, an ease that ever
Remembers her to my unfailing fever,
How she came forward to me, letting fall
Lamplight upon her dress till every small
Motion made visible seemed no mere endeavor
Of body to articulate its offer,
But more a grace won by the way from all
Striving in what is difficult, from all
Losses, so that she moved but to discover
A practice of the blood, as the gulls hover,
Winged with their life, above the harbor wall,
Tracing inflected silence in the tall
Air with a tilt of mastery and quiver
Against the light, as the light fell to favor
Her coming forth; this chiefly I recall.

It is a part of pride, guiding the hand
At the piano in the splash and passage
Of sacred dolphins, making numbers human
By sheer extravagance that can command
Pythagorean heavens to spell their message
Of some unlooked-for peace, out of the common;
Taking no thought at all that man and woman,
Lost in the trance of lamplight, felt the presage
Of the unbidden terror and bone hand
Of gracelessness, and the unspoken omen
That yet shall render all, by its first usage,
Speechless, inept, and totally unmanned.

LA CONDITION BOTANIQUE

Romans, rheumatic, gouty, came
To bathe in Ischian springs where water steamed,
Puffed and enlarged their bold imperial thoughts, and which
Later Madame Curie declared to be so rich
  In radioactive content as she deemed
    Should win them everlasting fame.

Scattered throughout their ice and snow
  The Finns have built airtight cabins of log
Where they may lie, limp and entranced by the sedative purr
Of steam pipes, or torment themselves with flails of fir
  To stimulate the blood, and swill down grog,
    Setting the particles aglow.

Similarly the Turks, but know
  Nothing of the more delicate thin sweat
Of plants, breathing their scented oxygen upon
Brooklyn's botanical gardens, roofed with glass and run
  So to the pleasure of each leafy pet,
    Manured, addressed in Latin, so

To its thermostatic happiness—
  Spreading its green and innocence to the ground
Where pipes, like Satan masquerading as the snake,
Coil and uncoil their frightful liquid length, and make
  Gurglings of love mixed with a rumbling sound
    Of sharp intestinal distress—

So to its pleasure, as I said,
  That each particular vegetable may thrive,
Early and late, as in the lot first given Man,
Sans interruption, as when Universal Pan
  Led on the Eternal Spring. The spears of chive,
    The sensitive plant, showing its dread,

The Mexican flytrap, that can knit
Its quilled jaws pitilessly, and would hurt
A fly with pleasure, leading Riley's life in bed
Of peat moss and of chemicals, and is thoughtfully fed
    Flies for the entrée, flies for the dessert,
      Fruit flies for fruit, and all of it

    Administered as by a wife—
    Lilith our lady, patroness of plants,
Who sings, *Lullay myn lykyng, myn owyn dere derlyng*,
Madrigals nightly to the spiny stalk in sterling
    Whole notes of admiration and romance—
      This, then, is what is called The Life.

    And we, like disinherited heirs,
    Old Adams, can inspect the void estate
At visiting hours: the unconditional garden spot,
The effortless innocence preserved, for God knows what,
    And think, as we depart by the toll gate:
      No one has lived here these five thousand years.

    Our world is turned on points, is whirled
    On wheels, Tibetan prayer wheels, French verb wheels,
The toothy wheels of progress, the terrible torque
Insisting, and in the sky, even above New York
    Rotate the marvelous four-fangled seals
      Ezekiel saw. The mother-of-pearled

    Home of the bachelor oyster lies
    Fondled in fluent shifts of bile and lime
As sunlight strikes the water, and it is of our world,
And will appear to us sometime where the finger is curled
    Between the frets upon a mandolin,
      Fancy cigar boxes, and eyes

Of ceremonial masks; and all
The places where Kilroy inscribed his name,
For instance, the ladies' rest room in the Gare du Nord,
The iron rump of Buddha, whose hallowed, hollowed core
    Admitted tourists once but all the same
        Housed a machine gun, and let fall

    A killing fire from its eyes
During the war; and Polyphemus hurled
Tremendous rocks that stand today off Sicily's coast
Signed with the famous scrawl of our most travelled ghost;
    And all these various things are of our world.
        But what's become of Paradise?

    Ah, it is lodged in glass, survives
In Brooklyn, like a throwback, out of style,
Like an incomprehensible veteran of the Grand
Army of the Republic in the reviewing stand
    Who sees young men in a mud-colored file
        March to the summit of their lives,

    For glory, for their country, with the flag
Joining divergent stars of North and South
In one blue field of heaven, till they fall in blood
And are returned at last unto their native mud—
    The eyes weighed down with stones, the sometimes mouth
        Helpless to masticate or gag

    Its old inheritance of earth.
In the sweat of thy face shalt thou manage, said the Lord.
And we, old Adams, stare through the glass panes and wince,
Fearing to see the ancestral apple, pear, or quince,
    The delicacy of knowledge, the fleshed Word,
        The globe of wisdom that was worth

Our lives, or so our parents thought,
And turn away to strengthen our poor breath
And body, keep the flesh rosy with hopeful dreams,
Peach-colored, practical, to decorate the bones, with schemes
Of life insurance, Ice-Cream-After-Death,
Hormone injections, against the *mort'*

Saison, largely to babble praise
Of Simeon Pyrites, patron saint
Of our Fools' Paradise, whose glittering effigy
Shines in God's normal sunlight till the blind men see
Visions as permanent as artists paint:
The body's firm, nothing decays

Upon the heirloom set of bones
In their gavotte. Yet we look through the glass
Where green lies ageless under snow-stacked roofs in steam-
Fitted apartments, and reflect how bud and stem
Are wholly flesh, and the immaculate grass
Does without buttressing of bones.

In open field or public bed
With ultraviolet help, man hopes to learn
The leafy secret, pay his most outstanding debt
To God in the salt and honesty of his sweat,
And in his streaming face manly to earn
His daily and all-nourishing bread.

JAPAN

It was a miniature country once
To my imagination; Home of the Short,
And also the academy of stunts
     Where acrobats are taught
  The famous secrets of the trade:
  To cycle in the big parade
While spinning plates upon their parasols,
Or somersaults that do not touch the ground,
     Or tossing seven balls
In Most Celestial Order round and round.

A child's quick sense of the ingenious stamped
All their invention: toys I used to get
At Christmastime, or the peculiar, cramped
     Look of their alphabet.
  Fragile and easily destroyed,
  Those little boats of celluloid
Driven by camphor round the bathroom sink,
And delicate the folded paper prize
     Which, dropped into a drink
Of water, grew up right before your eyes.

Now when we reached them it was with a sense
Sharpened for treachery compounding in their brains
Like mating weasels; our Intelligence
     Said: The Black Dragon reigns
  Secretly under yellow skin,
  Deeper than dyes of atabrine
And deadlier. The War Department said:
Remember you are Americans; forsake
     The wounded and the dead
At your own cost; remember Pearl and Wake.

And yet they bowed us in with ceremony,
Told us what brands of Sake were the best,
Explained their agriculture in a phony
    Dialect of the West,
  Meant vaguely to be understood
  As a shy sign of brotherhood
In the old human bondage to the facts
Of day-to-day existence. And like ants,
    Signaling tiny pacts
With their antennae, they would wave their hands.

At last we came to see them not as glib
Walkers of tightropes, worshipers of carp,
Nor yet a species out of Adam's rib
    Meant to preserve its warp
  In Cain's own image. They had learned
  That their tough eye-born goddess burned
Adoring fingers. They were very poor.
The holy mountain was not moved to speak.
    Wind at the paper door
Offered them snow out of its hollow peak.

Human endeavor clumsily betrays
Humanity. Their excrement served in this;
For, planting rice in water, they would raise
    Schistosomiasis
  Japonica, that enters through
  The pores into the avenue
And orbit of the blood, where it may foil
The heart and kill, or settle in the brain.
    This fruit of their nightsoil
Thrives in the skull, where it is called insane.

Now the quaint early image of Japan
That was so charming to me as a child
Seems like a bright design upon a fan,
    Of water rushing wild
  On rocks that can be folded up,
  A river which the wrist can stop
With a neat flip, revealing merely sticks
And silk of what had been a fan before,
    And like such winning tricks,
It shall be buried in excelsior.

LE MASSEUR DE MA SOEUR

I

My demoiselle, the cats are in the street,
Making a shrill cantata to their kind,
Accomplishing their furry, vigorous feat,
And I observe you shiver at it. You
Would rather have their little guts preserved
In the sweet excellence of a string quartet.
But, speaking for myself, I do not mind
This boisterous endeavor; it can do
Miracles for a lady who's unnerved
By the rude leanings of a family pet.

II

What Argus could not see was not worth seeing.
The fishy slime of his one hundred eyes
Shimmered all over his entire being
To lubricate his vision. A Voyeur
Of the first order, he would hardly blench
At the fine calculations of your dress.
Doubtless the moonlight or the liquor lies
Somewhere beneath this visible *bonheur*,
Yet I would freely translate from the French
The labials of such fleet happiness.

III

"If youth were all, our plush minority
Would lack no instrument to trick it out;
All cloth would emphasize it; not a bee
Could lecture us in offices of bliss.
Then all the appetites, arranged in rows,
Would dance cotillions absolute as ice
In high decorum rather than in rout."
He answered her, "Youth wants no emphasis,
But in extravagance of nature shows
A rigor more demanding than precise."

IV

"Pride is an illness rising out of pain,"
Said the ensnaffled Fiend who would not wince.
Does the neat corollary then obtain,
Humility comes burgeoning from pleasure?
Ah, masters, such a calculus is foul,
Of no more substance than a wasting cloud.
I cannot frame a logic to convince
Your honors of the urgent lawless measure
Of love, the which is neither fish nor fowl.
The meekest rise to tumble with the proud.

V

Goliath lies upon his back in Hell.
Out of his nostrils march a race of men,
Each with a little spear of hair; they yell,
"Attack the goat! O let us smite the goat!"
(An early German vision.) They are decked
With horns and beards and trappings of the brute
Capricorn, who remarked their origin.
Love, like a feather in a Roman throat,
Returned their suppers. They could not connect
Sentiment with a craving so acute.

VI

Those paragraphs most likely to arouse
Pear-shaped nuances to an ovoid brain,
Upstanding nipples under a sheer blouse,
Wink from the bold original, and keep
Their wicked parlance to confound the lewd
American, deftly obscured from sin
By the Fig-Leaf Edition of Montaigne.
But "summer nights were not devised for sleep,"
And who can cipher out, however shrewd,
The Man-in-the-Moon's microcephalic grin?

AS PLATO SAID

These public dances and other exercises of the
young maidens naked, in the sight of the young
men, were moreover incentives to marriage; and
to use Plato's expression, drew them almost as
necessarily by the attraction of love as a geo-
metrical conclusion is drawn from the premises.   PLUTARCH

Although I do not not know your name, although
It was a silly dance you did with apple flowers
Bunched in your hands after the racing games,
My friends and I have spent these several hours
Watching. Although I do not know your name,
I saw the sun dress half of you with shadow, and I saw
The wind water your eyes as though with tears
Until they flashed like newly-pointed spears.
This afternoon there was a giant daw
Turning above us—though I put no trust
In all these flying omens, being just
A plain man and a warrior, like my friends—
Yet I am mastered by uncommon force
And made to think of you, although it blends
Not with my humor, or the businesses
Of soldiering. I have seen a horse
Moving with more economy, and know
Armor is surer than a girl's promises.
But it is a compelling kind of law
Puts your design before me, even though
I put no faith or fancy in that daw
Turning above us. There's some rigor here,
More than in nature's daily masterpiece
That brings for us, with absolute and clear
Insistence, worms from their midnight soil,
Ungodly honk and trumpeting of geese
In the early morning, and at last the toil
Of soldiering. This is a simple code,
Far simpler than Lycurgus has set down.

The sheep come out of the hills, the sheep come down
When it rains, or gather under a tree,
And in the damp they stink most heartily.
Yet the hills are not so tough but they will yield
Brass for the kitchen, and the soft wet hair
Of the sheep will occupy some fingers. In the bottom fields
The herd's deposit shall assist the spring
Out of the earth and up into the air.
No. There is not a more unbending thing
In nature. It is an order that shall find
You out. There's not a season or a bird can bring
You to my senses or so harness me
To my intention. Let the Helots mind
The barley fields, lest they should see a daw
Turning to perch on some adjacent tree
And fancy it their sovereign ruler. No.
However we are governed, it shall draw
Both of us to its own conclusion, though
I do not even know you by your name.

DISCOURSE CONCERNING TEMPTATION

Though learned men have been at some dispute
Touching the taste and color, nature, name
And properties of the Original Fruit,
The bees that in midsummer congress swarm
In futile search of apple blossoms can
Testify to a sweetness such as man
Fears in his freezing heart, yet it could warm
Winter away, and redden the cheek with shame.

There was a gentleman of severest taste
Who won from wickedness by consummate strife
A sensibility suitable to his chaste
Formula. He found the world too lavish.
Temptation was his constant, intimate foe,
Constantly to be overcome by force, and so
His formula (fearing lest the world ravish
His senses) applied the rigors of art to life.

But in recurrent dreams saw himself dead,
Mourned by chrysanthemums that walked about,
Each bending over him its massive head
And weeping on him such sweet tender tears
That as each drop spattered upon his limbs
Green plant life blossomed in that place. For hymns
Marking his mean demise, his frigid ears
Perceived the belch of frogs, low and devout.

The problem is not simple. In Guadeloupe
The fer-de-lance displays his ugly trait
Deep in the sweaty undergrowth where droop
Pears of a kind not tasted, where depend
Strange apples, in the shade of *Les Mamelles*.
The place is neither Paradise nor Hell,
But of their divers attributes a blend:
It is man's brief and natural estate.

SAMUEL SEWALL

Samuel Sewall, in a world of wigs,
Flouted opinion in his personal hair;
For foppery he gave not any figs,
But in his right and honor took the air.

Thus in his naked style, though well attired,
He went forth in the city, or paid court
To Madam Winthrop, whom he much admired,
Most godly, but yet liberal with the port.

And all the town admired for two full years
His excellent address, his gifts of fruit,
Her gracious ways and delicate white ears,
And held the course of nature absolute.

But yet she bade him suffer a peruke,
"That One be not distinguished from the All";
Delivered of herself this stern rebuke
Framed in the resonant language of St. Paul.

"Madam," he answered her, "I have a Friend
Furnishes me with hair out of His strength,
And He requires only I attend
Unto His charity and to its length."

And all the town was witness to his trust:
On Monday he walked out with the Widow Gibbs,
A pious lady of charm and notable bust,
Whose heart beat tolerably beneath her ribs.

On Saturday he wrote proposing marriage,
And closed, imploring that she be not cruel,
"Your favorable answer will oblige,
Madam, your humble servant, Samuel Sewall."

DRINKING SONG

A toast to that lady over the fireplace
Who wears a snood of pearls. Her eyes are turned
Away from the posterity that loosed
Drunken invaders to the living room,
Toppled the convent bell-tower, and burned
The sniper-ridden outhouses. The face
Of Beatrice d'Este, reproduced
In color, offers a profile to this dark,
Hand-carved interior. High German gloom
Flinches before our boots upon the desk
Where the *Ortsgruppenführer* used to park
His sovereign person. Not a week ago
The women of this house went down among
The stacked-up kindling wood, the picturesque,
Darkening etchings of Vesuvius,
Piled mattresses upon themselves, and shook,
And prayed to God in their guttural native tongue
For mercy, forgiveness, and the death of us.

We are indeed diminished.
                                    We are twelve.
But have recaptured a sufficiency
Of France's cognac; and it shall be well,
Given sufficient time, if we can down
Half of it, being as we are, reduced.
Five dead in the pasture, yet they loom
As thirstily as ever. Are recalled
By daring wagers to this living room:
"I'll be around to leak over your grave."

And *Durendal*, my only *Durendal*,
Thou hast preserved me better than a sword;
Rest in the enemy umbrella stand
While that I measure out another drink.
I am beholden to thee, by this hand,
This measuring hand. We are beholden all.

A POEM FOR JULIA

Held in her hand of "almost flawless skin"
A small sprig of Sweet William as a badge
Of beauty, and the region of her nose
Seemed to be made so delicate and thin,
Light of the sun might touch the cartilage
With numerous golden tones and hints of rose
If she but turned to the window now to smell
The lilacs and the undulant green lawn,
Trim as a golf course, where a haze revealed
The sheep, distinguished each with a separate bell,
Grazing and moping near the neighbor field
Where all the clover-seeking bees were gone,
But stood in modesty in the full sight
Of Memling, whose accomplished busy hand
Rendered this wimpled lady in such white
Untinted beauty, that she seems to stand
Even as gently to our present gaze
As she had stood there in her breathing days.

Seeing this painting, I am put in mind
Of many a freakish harridan and clown
Who by their native clumsiness or fate
Won for themselves astonishing renown
And stand amongst us even to this date
Since art and history were so inclined:
Here, in a generous Italian scene,
A pimpled, chinless shepherd, whose rough thought
And customary labor lead the ram
Into his sheep for profit and for sport,
Guide their ungainly pleasure with obscene
Mirth at the comedy of sire and dam
Till he has grossly married every ewe—
This shepherd, in a mangy cap of fur,
Stands at the window still regarding her,
That only lady, if the Pope speaks true,
Who with a grace more than we understand
Ate of her portion with a flawless hand.

And once a chattering agent of Pope Paul,
A small, foul-minded clergyman, stood by
To watch the aging Michelangelo
Set his *Last Judgment* on the papal wall,
And muttered thereupon that to his eye
It was a lewd and most indecent show
Of nakedness, not for a sacred place,
Fitted to whorehouse or to public bath;
At which the painter promptly drew his face
Horribly gripped, his face a fist of pain,
Amongst those fixed in God's eternal wrath,
And when the fool made motion to complain
He earned this solemn judgment of the Pope:
"Had art set you on Purgatory's Mount
Then had I done my utmost for your hope,
But Hell's fierce immolation takes no count
Of offices and prayers, for as you know,
From that place *nulla est redemptio.*"

And I recall certain ambassadors,
Cuffed all in ermine and with vests of mail
Who came their way into the town of Prague
Announced by horns, as history tells the tale,
To seek avoidances of future wars
And try the meaning of the Decalogue,
But whispers went about against their names.
And so it happened that a courtier-wit,
Hating their cause with an intemperate might,
Lauded his castle's vantage, and made claims
Upon their courtesy to visit it,
And having brought them to that famous height
To witness the whole streamed and timbered view
Of his ancestral property, and smell
His fine ancestral air, he pushed them through
The open-standing window, whence they fell,
Oh, in a manner worthy to be sung,
Full thirty feet into a pile of dung.

How many poets, with profoundest breath,
Have set their ladies up to spite the worm,
So that pale mistress or high-busted bawd
Could smile and spit into the eye of death
And dance into our midst all fleshed and firm
Despite she was most perishably flawed?
She lasts, but not in her own body's right,
Nor do we love her for her endless poise.
All of her beauty has become a part
Of neighboring beauty, and what could excite
High expectations among hopeful boys
Now leaves her to the nunnery of art.
And yet a searching discipline can keep
That eye still clear, as though in spite of Hell,
So that she seems as innocent as sheep
Where they still graze, denuded of their smell,
Where fool still writhes upon the chapel wall,
A shepherd stares, ambassadors still fall.

Adam and Eve knew such perfection once,
God's finger in the cloud, and on the ground
Nothing but springtime, nothing else at all.
But in our fallen state where the blood hunts
For blood, and rises at the hunting sound,
What do we know of lasting since the fall?
Who has not, in the oil and heat of youth,
Thought of the flourishing of the almond tree,
The grasshopper, and the failing of desire,
And thought his tongue might pierce the secrecy
Of the six-pointed starlight, and might choir
A secret-voweled, unutterable truth?
The heart is ramified with an old force
(Outlingering the blood, out of the sway
Of its own fleshy trap) that finds its source
Deep in the phosphorous waters of the bay,
Or in the wind, or pointing cedar tree,
Or its own ramified complexity.

CHRISTMAS IS COMING

Darkness is for the poor, and thorough cold,
As they go wandering the hills at night,
Gunning for enemies. Winter locks the lake;
The rocks are harder for it. What was grass
Is fossilized and brittle; it can hurt,
Being a torture to the kneeling knee,
And in the general pain of cold, it sticks
Particular pain where crawling is required.

> *Christmas is coming. The goose is getting fat.*
> *Please put a penny in the Old Man's hat.*

Where is the warmth of blood? The enemy
Has ears that can hear clearly in the cold,
Can hear the shattering of fossil grass,
Can hear the stiff cloth rub against itself,
Making a sound. Where is the blood? It lies
Locked in the limbs of some poor animal
In a diaspora of crimson ice.
The skin freezes to metal. One must crawl
Quietly in the dark. Where is the warmth?
The lamb has yielded up its fleece and warmth
And woolly life, but who shall taste of it?
Here on the ground one cannot see the stars.
The lamb is killed. *The goose is getting fat.*
A wind blows steadily against the trees,
And somewhere in the blackness they are black.
Yet crawling one encounters bits of string,
Pieces of foil left by the enemy.
(A rifle takes its temper from the cold.)
Where is the pain? The sense has frozen up,
And fingers cannot recognize the grass,
Cannot distinguish their own character,
Being blind with cold, being stiffened by the cold;
Must find out thistles to remember pain.
Keep to the frozen ground or else be killed.

Yet crawling one encounters in the dark
The frosty carcasses of birds, their feet
And wings all glazed. And still we crawl to learn
Where pain was lost, how to recover pain.
Reach for the brambles, crawl to them and reach,
Clutching for thorns, search carefully to feel
The point of thorns, life's crown, *the Old Man's hat.*
Yet quietly. Do not disturb the brambles.
Winter has taught the air to clarify
All noises, and the enemy can hear
Perfectly in the cold. Nothing but sound
Is known. Where is the warmth and pain?
Christmas is coming. Darkness is for the poor.

If you haven't got a penny, a ha'penny will do,
If you haven't got a ha'penny, God bless you.

IMITATION

Let men take note of her, touching her shyness,
How grace informs and presses the brocade
Wherein her benefits are whitely stayed,
And think all glittering enterprise, and highness
Of blood or deed were yet in something minus
Lacking the wide approval of her mouth,
And to betoken every man his drouth,
Drink, in her name, all tankards to their dryness.

Wanting her clear perfection, how may tongues
Manifest what no language understands?
Yet as her beauty evermore commands
Even the tanager with tiny lungs
To flush all silence, may she by these songs
Know it was love I looked for at her hands.

THE GARDENS OF THE VILLA D'ESTE

This is Italian. Here
Is cause for the undiminished bounce
Of sex, cause for the lark, the animal spirit
To rise, aerated, but not beyond our reach, to spread
Friction upon the air, cause to sing loud for the bed
Of jonquils, the linen bed, and established merit
Of love, and grandly to pronounce
Pleasure without peer.

Goddess, be with me now;
Commend my music to the woods.
There is no garden to the practiced gaze
Half so erotic: here the sixteenth century thew
Rose to its last perfection, this being chiefly due
To the provocative role the water plays.
Tumble and jump, the fountains' moods
Teach the world how.

But, ah, who ever saw
Finer proportion kept. The sum
Of intersecting limbs was something planned.
Ligorio, the laurel! Every turn and quirk
Weaves in this waving green and liquid world to work
Its formula, binding upon the gland,
Even as molecules succumb
To Avogadro's law.

The intricate mesh of trees,
Sagging beneath a lavender snow
Of wisteria, wired by creepers, perfectly knit
A plot to capture alive the migrant, tourist soul
In its corporeal home with all the deft control
And artifice of an Hephaestus' net.
Sunlight and branch rejoice to show
Sudden interstices.

The whole garden inclines
The flesh as water falls, to seek
For depth. Consider the top balustrade,
Where twinned stone harpies, with domed and virgin breasts,
Spurt from their nipples that no pulse or hand has pressed
Clear liquid arcs of benefice and aid
To the chief purpose. They are Greek
Versions of valentines

And spend themselves to fill
The celebrated flumes that skirt
The horseshoe stairs. Triumphant then to a sluice,
With Brownian movement down the giggling water drops
Past haunches, over ledges, out of mouths, and stops
In a still pool, but, by a plumber's ruse,
Rises again to laugh and squirt
At heaven, and is still

Busy descending. White
Ejaculations leap to teach
How fertile are these nozzles; the streams run
Góngora through the garden, channel themselves, and pass
To lily-padded ease, where insubordinate lass
And lad can cool their better parts, where sun
Heats them again to furnace pitch
To prove his law is light.

Marble the fish that puke
Eternally, marble the lips
Of gushing naiads, pleased to ridicule
Adonis, marble himself, and larger than life-sized,
Untouched by Venus, posthumously circumcised
Patron of Purity; and any fool
Who feels no flooding at the hips
These spendthrift stones rebuke.

It was in such a place
That Mozart's Figaro contrived
The totally expected. This is none
Of your French topiary, geometric works,
Based on God's rational, wrist-watch universe; here lurks
   The wood louse, the night crawler, the homespun
      Spider; here are they born and wived
         And bedded, by God's grace.

Actually, it is real
The way the world is real: the horse
Must turn against the wind, and the deer feed
Against the wind, and finally the garden must allow
For the recalcitrant; a style can teach us how
   To know the world in little where the weed
      Has license, where by dint of force
         D'Estes have set their seal.

Their spirit entertains.
And we are honorable guests
Come by imagination, come by night,
Hearing in the velure of darkness impish strings
Mincing Tartini, hearing the hidden whisperings:
   "*Carissima*, the moon gives too much light,"
      Though by its shining it invests
         Her bodice with such gains

As show their shadowed worth
Deep in the cleavage. Lanterns, lamps
Of pumpkin-colored paper dwell upon
The implications of the skin-tight silk, allude
Directly to the body; under the subdued
   Report of corks, whisperings, the *chaconne*,
      Boisterous water runs its ramps
         Out, to the end of mirth.

Accommodating plants
Give umbrage where the lovers delve
Deeply for love, give way to their delight,
As Pliny's pregnant mouse, bearing unborn within her
Lewd sons and pregnant daughters, hears the adept beginner:
"*Cor mio*, your supports are much too tight,"
While overhead the stars resolve
Every extravagance.

Tomorrow, before dawn,
Gardeners will come to resurrect
Downtrodden iris, dispose of broken glass,
Return the diamond earrings to the villa, but
As for the moss upon the statue's shoulder, not
To defeat its green invasion, but to pass
Over the liberal effect
Caprice and cunning spawn.

For thus it was designed:
Controlled disorder at the heart
Of everything, the paradox, the old
Oxymoronic itch to set the formal strictures
Within a natural context, where the tension lectures
Us on our mortal state, and by controlled
Disorder, labors to keep art
From being too refined.

Susan, it had been once
My hope to see this place with you,
See it as in the hour of thoughtless youth.
For age mocks all diversity, its genesis,
And whispers to the heart, "*Cor mio*, beyond all this
Lies the unchangeable and abstract truth,"
Claims of the grass, it is not true,
And makes our youth its dunce.

Therefore, some later day
Recall these words, let them be read
Between us, let them signify that here
Are more than formulas, that age sees no more clearly
For its poor eyesight, and philosophy grows surly,
That falling water and the blood's career
Lead down the garden path to bed
And win us both to May.

A DEEP BREATH AT DAWN

Morning has come at last. The rational light
Discovers even the humblest thing that yearns
For heaven; from its scaled and shadeless height,
Figures its difficult way among the ferns,
Nests in the trees, and is ambitious to warm
The chilled vein, and to light the spider's thread
With modulations hastening to a storm
Of the full spectrum, rushing from red to red.
I have watched its refinements since the dawn,
When, at the birdcall, all the ghosts were gone.

The wolf, the fig tree, and the woodpecker
Were sacred once to Undertaker Mars;
Honor was done in Rome to that home-wrecker
Whose armor and whose ancient, toughened scars
Made dance the very meat of Venus' heart,
And hot her ichor, and immense her eyes,
Till his rough ways and her invincible art
Locked and laid low their shining, tangled thighs.
My garden yields his fig tree, even now
Bearing heraldic fruit at every bough.

Someone I have not seen for six full years
Might pass this garden through, and might pass by
The oleander bush, the bitter pears
Unfinished by the sun, with only an eye
For the sun-speckled shade of the fig tree,
And shelter in its gloom, and raise his hand
For tribute and for nourishment (for he
Was once entirely at the god's command)
But that his nature, being all undone,
Cannot abide the clarity of the sun.

Morning deceived him those six years ago.
Morning swam in the pasture, being all green
And yellow, and the swallow coiled in slow
Passage of dials and spires above the scene
Cluttered with dandelions, near the fence
Where the hens strutted redheaded and wreathed
With dark, imponderable chicken sense,
Hardly two hundred yards from where he breathed,
And where, from their declamatory roosts,
The cocks cried brazenly against all ghosts.

Warmth in the milling air, the warmth of blood;
The dampness of the earth; the forest floor
Of fallen needles, the dried and creviced mud,
Lay matted and caked with sunlight, and the war
Seemed elsewhere; light impeccable, unmixed,
Made accurate the swallow's traveling print
Over the pasture, till he saw it fixed
Perfectly on a little patch of mint.
And he could feel in his body, driven home,
The wild tooth of the wolf that suckled Rome.

What if he came and stood beside my tree,
A poor, transparent thing with nothing to do,
His chest showing a jagged vacancy
Through which I might admire the distant view?
My house is solid, and the windows house
In their fine membranes the gelatinous light,
But darkness follows, and the dark allows
Obscure hints of a tapping sound at night.
And yet it may be merely that I dream
A woodpecker attacks the attic beam.

It is as well the light keeps him away;
We should have little to say in days like these,
Although once friends. We should have little to say,
But that there will be much planting of fig trees,
And Venus shall be clad in the prim leaf,
And turn a solitary. And her god, forgot,
Cast by that emblem out, shall spend his grief
Upon us. In that day the fruit shall rot
Unharvested. Then shall the sullen god
Perform his mindless fury in our blood.

A ROMAN HOLIDAY

I write from Rome. Last year, the Holy Year,
The flock was belled, and pilgrims came to see
How milkweed mocked the buried engineer,
Wedging between his marble works, where free
And famished went the lions forth to tear
A living meal from the offending knee,
And where, on pagan ground, turned to our good,
Santa Maria sopra Minerva stood.

And came to see where Caesar Augustus turned
Brick into marble, thus to celebrate
Apollo's Peace, that lately had been learned,
And where the Rock that bears the Church's weight,
Crucified Peter, raised his eyes and yearned
For final sight of heavenly estate,
But saw ungainly huge above his head
Our stony base to which the flesh is wed.

And see the wealthy, terraced Palatine,
Where once the unknown god or goddess ruled
In mystery and silence, whose divine
Name has been lost or hidden from the fooled,
Daydreaming employee who guards the shrine
And has forgotten how men have been schooled
To hide the Hebrew Vowels, that craft or sin
Might not pronounce their sacred origin.

And has forgot that on the temple floor
Once was a Vestal Virgin overcome
Even by muscle of the god of war,
And ran full of unearthly passion home,
Being made divinity's elected whore
And fertile with the twins that founded Rome.
Columns are down. Unknown the ruined face
Of travertine, found in a swampy place.

Yet there was wisdom even then that said,
Nothing endures at last but only One;
Sands shift in the wind, petals are shed,
Eternal cities also are undone;
Informed the living and the pious dead
That there is no new thing under the sun,
Nor can the best ambition come to good
When it is founded on a brother's blood.

I write from Rome. It is late afternoon
Nearing the Christmas season. Blooded light
Floods through the Colosseum, where platoon
And phalanx of the Lord slaved for the might
Of Titus' pleasure. Blood repeats its tune
Loudly against my eardrums as I write,
And recollects what they were made to pay
Who out of worship put their swords away.

The bells declare it. "Crime is at the base,"
Rings in the belfry where the blood is choired.
Crime stares from the unknown, ruined face,
And the cold wind, endless and wrath-inspired,
Cries out for judgment in a swampy place
As darkness claims the trees. "Blood is required,
And it shall fall," below the Seven Hills
The blood of Remus whispers out of wells.

ALCESTE IN THE WILDERNESS

> *Non, je ne puis souffrir cette lâche méthode*
> *Qu'affectent la plupart de vos gens à la mode . . .*
> MOLIERE: *Le Misanthrope*

Evening is clogged with gnats as the light fails,
And branches bloom with gold and copper screams
Of birds with figured and sought-after tails
To plume a lady's gear; the motet wails
Through Africa upon dissimilar themes.

A little snuffbox whereon Daphnis sings
In pale enamels, touching love's defeat,
Calls up the color of her underthings
And plays upon the taut memorial strings,
Trailing her laces down into this heat.

One day he found, topped with a smutty grin,
The small corpse of a monkey, partly eaten.
Force of the sun had split the bluish skin,
Which, by their questioning and entering in,
A swarm of bees had been concerned to sweeten.

He could distill no essence out of this.
That yellow majesty and molten light
Should bless this carcass with a sticky kiss
Argued a brute and filthy emphasis.
The half-moons of the fingernails were white,

And where the nostrils opened on the skies,
Issuing to the sinus, where the ant
Crawled swiftly down to undermine the eyes
Of cloudy aspic, nothing could disguise
How terribly the thing looked like Philinte.

Will-o'-the-wisp, on the scum-laden water,
Burns in the night, a gaseous deceiver,
In the pale shade of France's foremost daughter.
Heat gives his thinking cavity no quarter,
For he is burning with the monkey's fever.

Before the bees have diagrammed their comb
Within the skull, before summer has cracked
The back of Daphnis, naked, polychrome,
Versailles shall see the tempered exile home,
Peruked and stately for the final act.

MILLIONS OF STRANGE SHADOWS

For H E L E N

of whom I have
Receiv'd a second life . . .

THE COST

Why, let the stricken deer go weep,
The hart ungallèd play . . .

Think how some excellent, lean torso hugs
      The brink of weight and speed,
Coasting the margins of those rival tugs
      Down the thin path of friction,
The athlete's dancing vectors, the spirit's need,
      And muscle's cleanly diction,

Clean as a Calder, whose interlacing ribs
      Depend on one another,
Or a keen heeling of tackle, fluttering jibs
      And slotted centerboards,
A fleet of breasting gulls riding the smother
      And puzzle of heaven's wards.

Instinct with joy, a young Italian banks
      Smoothly around the base
Of Trajan's column, feeling between his flanks
      That cool, efficient beast,
His Vespa, at one with him in a centaur's race,
      Fresh from a Lapith feast,

And his Lapith girl behind him. Both of them lean
      With easy nonchalance
Over samphire-tufted cliffs which, though unseen,
      Are known, as the body knows
New risks and tilts, terrors and loves and wants,
      Deeply inside its clothes.

She grips the animal-shouldered naked skin
      Of his fitted leather jacket,
Letting a wake of hair float out the spin
      And dazzled rinse of air,
Yet for all their headlong lurch and flatulent racket
      They seem to loiter there,

Forever aslant in their moment and the mind's eye.
      Meanwhile, around the column
There also turn, and turn eternally,
      Two thousand raw recruits
And scarred veterans coiling the stone in solemn
      Military pursuits,

The heft and grit of the emperors' Dacian Wars
      That lasted fifteen years.
All of that youth and purpose is, of course,
      No more than so much dust.
And even Trajan, of his imperial peers
      Accounted "the most just,"

Honored by Dante, by Gregory the Great
      Saved from eternal Hell,
Swirls in the motes kicked up by the cough and spate
      Of the Vespa's blue exhaust,
And a voice whispers inwardly, "My soul,
      It is the cost, the cost,"

Like some unhinged Othello, who's just found out
      That justice is no more,
While Cassio, Desdemona, Iago shout
      Like true Venetians all,
"Go screw yourself; all's fair in love and war!"
      And the bright standards fall.

Better they should not hear that whispered phrase,
      The young Italian couple;
Surely the mind in all its brave assays
      Must put much thinking by,
To be, as Yeats would have it, free and supple
      As a long-legged fly.

Look at their slender purchase, how they list
      Like a blown clipper, brought
To the lively edge of peril, to the kissed
      Lip, the victor's crown,
The prize of life. Yet one unbodied thought
      Could topple them, bring down

The whole shebang. And why should they take thought
      Of all that ancient pain,
The Danube winters, the nameless young who fought,
      The blood's uncertain lease?
Or remember that that fifteen-year campaign
      Won seven years of peace?

BLACK BOY IN THE DARK

for Thomas Cornell

Peace, tawny slave, half me and half thy dam!
Did not thy hue bewray whose brat thou art,
. . .
Villain, thou mightst have been an emperor.

Summer. A hot, moth-populated night.
Yesterday's maples in the village park
Are boxed away into the vaults of dark,
To be returned tomorrow, like our flag,
Which was brought down from its post office height
At sunset, folded, and dumped in a mailbag.

Wisdom, our Roman matron, perched on her throne
In front of the library, the Civil War
Memorial (History and Hope) no more
Are braced, trustworthy figures. Some witching skill
Softly dismantled them, stone by heavy stone,
And the small town, like Bethlehem, lies still.

And it is still at the all-night service station,
Where Andy Warhol's primary colors shine
In simple commercial glory, the Esso sign
Revolving like a funland lighthouse, where
An eighteen-year-old black boy clocks the nation,
Reading a comic book in a busted chair.

Our solitary guardian of the law
Of diminishing returns? The President,
Addressing the first contingent of draftees sent
To Viet Nam, was brief: "Life is not fair,"
He said, and was right, of course. Everyone saw
What happened to him in Dallas. We were there,

We suffered, we were Whitman. And now the boy
Daydreams about the White House, the rising shares
Of Standard Oil, the whited sepulchres.
But what, after all, has he to complain about,
This expendable St. Michael we employ
To stay awake and keep the darkness out?

AN AUTUMNAL

The lichens, like a gorgeous, soft disease
      In rust and gold rosette
Emboss the bouldered wall, and creepers seize
      In their cup-footed fret,

Ravelled and bare, such purchase as affords.
      The sap-tide slides to ebb,
And leafstems, like the drumsticks of small birds,
      Lie snagged in a spiderweb.

Down at the stonework base, among the stump-
      Fungus and feather moss,
Dead leaves are sunken in a shallow sump
      Of energy and loss,

Enriched now with the colors of old coins
      And brilliance of wet leather.
An earthen tea distills at the roots-groins
      Into the smoky weather

A deep, familiar essence of the year:
      A sweet fetor, a ghost
Of foison, gently welcoming us near
      To humus, mulch, compost.

The last mosquitoes lazily hum and play
      Above the yeasting earth
A feeble *Gloria* to this cool decay
      Or casual dirge of birth.

"DICHTUNG UND WAHRHEIT"

for Cyrus Hoy

I

The Discus Thrower's marble heave,
  Captured in mid-career,
That polished poise, that Parian arm
  Sleeved only in the air,
Vesalian musculature, white
  As the mid-winter moon—
This, and the clumsy snapshot of
  An infantry platoon,
Those grubby and indifferent men,
  Lounging in bivouac,
Their rifles aimless in their laps,
  Stop history in its tracks.

We who are all aswim in time,
  We, "the inconstant ones,"
How can such fixture speak to us?
  The chisel and the lens
Deal in a taxidermy
  Of our arrested flights,
And by their brute translation we
  Turn into Benthamites.
Those soldiers, like some senior class,
  Were they prepared to dye
In silver nitrate images
  Behind the camera's eye?

It needs a Faust to animate
  The wan homunculus,
Construe the stark, unchanging text,
  Winkle the likes of us
Out of a bleak geology
  That art has put to rest,
And by a sacred discipline

Give breath back to the past.
How, for example, shall I read
The expression on my face
Among that company of men
In that unlikely place?

11

Easy enough to claim, in the dawn of hindsight,
That Mozart's music perfectly enacts
Pastries and powdered wigs, an architecture
Of white and gold rosettes, balanced parterres.
More difficult to know how the spirit learns
Its scales, or the exact dimensions of fear:
The nameless man dressed head-to-foot in black,
Come to commission a requiem in a hurry.
In the diatonic house there are many mansions:
A hunting lodge in the mountains, a peaceable
      cloister,
A first-class restaurant near the railroad yards,
But also a seedy alms-house, the granite prisons
And oubliettes of the soul. Just how such truth
Gets itself stated in pralltrillers and mordents
Not everyone can say. But the 'cellist,
Leaning over his labors, his eyes closed,
Is engaged in that study, blocking out, for the
      moment,
Audience, hall, and a great part of himself
In what, not wrongly, might be called research,
Or the most private kind of honesty.

We begin with the supreme donnée, the world,
Upon which every text is commentary,
And yet they play each other, the oak-leaf cured
In sodden ditches of autumn darkly confirms

Our words; and by the frailest trifles
(A doubt, a whisper, and a handkerchief)
Venetian pearl and onyx are cast away.
It is, in the end, the solitary scholar
Who returns us to the freshness of the text,
Which returns to us the freshness of the world
In which we find ourselves, like replicas,
Dazzled by glittering dawns, upon a stage.
Pentelic balconies give on the east;
The clouds are scrolled, bellied in apricot,
Adrift in pools of Scandinavian blue.
Light crisps the terraces of dolomite.
Enter The Prologue, who at once declares,
"We begin with the supreme donnée, the word."

A VOICE AT A SEANCE

It is rather strange to be speaking, but I know you are
     there
Wanting to know, as if it were worth knowing.
Nor is it important that I died in combat
In a good cause or an indifferent one.
Such things, it may surprise you, are not regarded.
Something too much of this.

You are bound to be disappointed,
Wanting to know, are there any trees?
It is all different from what you suppose,
And the darkness is not darkness exactly,
But patience, silence, withdrawal, the sad knowledge
That it was almost impossible not to hurt anyone
Whether by action or inaction.
At the beginning of course there was a sense of loss,
Not of one's own life, but of what seemed
The easy, desirable lives one might have led.
Fame or wealth are hard to achieve,
And goodness even harder;
But the cost of all of them is a familiar deformity
Such as everyone suffers from:
An allergy to certain foods, nausea at the sight of blood,
A slight impediment of speech, shame at one's own body,
A fear of heights or claustrophobia.
What you learn has nothing whatever to do with joy,
Nor with sadness, either. You are mostly silent.
You come to a gentle indifference about being thought
Either a fool or someone with valuable secrets.
It may be that the ultimate wisdom
Lies in saying nothing.
I think I may already have said too much.

GREEN: AN EPISTLE

This urge, wrestle, resurrection of dry sticks,
Cut stems struggling to put down feet,
What saint strained so much,
Rose on such lopped limbs to a new life?
                    THEODORE ROETHKE

         I write at last of the one forbidden topic
We, by a truce, have never touched upon:
Resentment, malice, hatred so inwrought
With moral inhibitions, so at odds with
The home-movie of yourself as patience, kindness,
And Charlton Heston playing Socrates,
That almost all of us were taken in,
Yourself not least, as to a giant Roxy,
Where the lights dimmed and the famous allegory
Of Good and Evil, clearly identified
By the unshaven surliness of the Bad Guys,
The virginal meekness of the ingénue,
Seduced us straight into that perfect world
Of Justice under God. Art for the sake
Of money, glamour, ego, self-deceit.
When we emerged into the assaulting sunlight,
We had a yen, like bad philosophers,
To go back to stay forever, there in the dark
With the trumpets, horses, and ancient Certitudes
On which, as we know, this great nation was founded,
Washington crossed the Delaware, and so forth.
And all of us, for an hour or so after,
Were Humphrey Bogart dating Ingrid Bergman,
Walking together but incommunicado
Till subway and homework knocked us out of it.
Yet even then, whatever we returned to
Was not, although we thought it was, the world.

         I write at last on this topic because I am safe
Here in this grubby little border town
With its one cheap hotel. No one has my address.

The food is bad, the wine is too expensive,
And the local cathedral marred by restorations.
But from my balcony I view the east
For miles and, if I lean, the local sunsets
That bathe a marble duke with what must be
Surely the saddest light I have ever seen.
The air is thin and cool at this elevation,
And my desk wobbles unless propped with
    matchbooks.

It began, I suppose, as a color, yellow-green,
The tincture of spring willows, not so much color
As the sensation of color, haze that took shape
As a light scum, a doily of minutiae
On the smooth pool and surface of your mind.
A founding colony, Pilgrim amoebas
Descended from the gaseous flux when Zeus
Tossed down his great original thunderbolt
That flashed in darkness like an electric tree
Or the lit-up veins in an old arthritic hand.

Here is the microscope one had as a child,
The Christmas gift of some forgotten uncle.
Here is the slide with a drop of cider vinegar
As clear as gin, clear as your early mind.
Look down, being most careful not to see
Your own eye in the mirror underneath,
Which will appear, unless your view is right,
As a darkness on the face of the first waters.
When all is silvery and brilliant, look:
The long, thin, darting shapes, the flagellates,
Rat-tailed, ambitious, lash themselves along—
Those humble, floating ones, those simple cells
Content to be borne on whatever tide,
Trustful, the very image of consent—
These are the frail, unlikely origins,
Scarcely perceived, of all you shall become.
Scarcely perceived? But at this early age

(What are you, one or two?) you have no
    knowledge,
Nor do your folks, nor could the gravest doctors
Suspect that anything was really wrong.
Nor see the pale beginnings, lace endeavors
That with advancing ages shall mature
Into sea lettuce, beard the rocky shore
With a light green of soft and tidal hair.

    Whole eras, seemingly without event,
Now scud the glassy pool processionally
Until one day, misty, uncalendared,
As mild and unemphatic as a schwa,
Vascular tissue, conduit filaments
Learn how to feed the outposts of that small
Emerald principate. Now there are roots,
The filmy gills of toadstools, crested fern,
Quillworts, and foxtail mosses, and at last
Snapweed, loment, trillium, grass, herb Robert.
How soundlessly, shyly this came about,
One thinks today. But that is not the truth.
It was, from the first, an everlasting war
Conducted, as always, at gigantic cost.
Think of the droughts, the shifts of wind and
    weather,
The many seeds washed to some salt conclusion
Or brought to rest at last on barren ground.
Think of some inching tendrils worming down
In hope of water, blind and white as death.
Think of the strange mutations life requires.
Only the toughest endured, themselves much
    altered,
Trained in the cripple's careful sciences
Of mute accommodation. The survivors
Were all, one way or another, amputees
Who learned to live with their stumps, like
    Brueghel's beggars.

Yet, for all that, it clearly was a triumph,
Considering, as one must, what was to come.
And, even by themselves, those fields of clover,
Cattails, marsh bracken, water-lily pads
Stirred by the lightest airs, pliant, submissive—
Who could have called their slow creation *rage*?

Consider, as one must, what was to come.
Great towering conifers, deciduous,
Rib-vaulted elms, the banyan, oak, and palm,
Sequoia forests of vindictiveness
That also would go down on the death list
And, buried deep beneath alluvial shifts,
Would slowly darken into lakes of coal
And then under exquisite pressure turn
Into the tiny diamonds of pure hate.
The delicate fingers of the clematis
Feeling their way along a face of shale
With all the ingenuity of spite.
The indigestible thistle of revenge.
And your most late accomplishment, the rose.
Until at last, what we might designate
As your Third Day, behold a world of green:
Color of hope, of the Church's springtide
    vestments,
The primal wash, heraldic hue of envy.
But in what pre-lapsarian disguise!
Strangers and those who do not know you well
(Yourself not least) are quickly taken in
By a summery prospect, shades of innocence.
Like that young girl, a sort of chance
    acquaintance,
Seven or eight she was, on the New York
    Central,
Who, with a blue-eyed, beatific smile,
Shouted with joy, "Look, Mommy, quick. Look.
    Daisies!"

These days, with most of us at a safe distance,
You scarcely know yourself. Whole weeks go by
Without your remembering that enormous effort,
Ages of disappointment, the long ache
Of motives twisted out of recognition,
The doubt and hesitation all submerged
In those first clear waters, that untroubled pool.
Who could have hoped for this eventual peace?
Moreover, there are moments almost of bliss,
A sort of recompense, in which your mood
Sorts with the peach endowments of late sunlight
On a snowfield or on the breaker's froth
Or the white steeple of the local church.
Or, like a sunbather, whose lids retain
A greenish, gemmed impression of the sun
In lively, fluctuant geometries,
You sometimes contemplate a single image,
Utterly silent, utterly at rest.
It is of someone, a stranger, quite unknown,
Sitting alone in a foreign-looking room,
Gravely intent at a table propped with match-
    books,
Writing this very poem—about me.

SOMEBODY'S LIFE

I

Cliff-high, sunlit, in the tawny warmth of youth,
He gazed down at the breakneck rocks below,
Entranced by the water's loose attacks of jade,
The sousing waves, the interminable, blind
Fury of scattered opals, flung tiaras,
Full, hoisted, momentary chandeliers.
He spent most of the morning there alone.
He smoked, recalled some lines of poetry,
Felt himself claimed by such rash opulence:
These were the lofty figures of his soul.
What was it moved him in all that swash and
     polish?
Against an imperial sky of lupine blue,
Suspended, as it seemed to him, forever,
Blazed a sun-flooded gem of the first water.

II

Blazed, as it seemed, forever. Was this the secret
Gaudery of self-love, or a blood-bidden,
Involuntary homage to the world?
As it happens, he was doomed never to know.
At times in darkened rooms he thought he heard
The soft ruckus of patiently torn paper,
The sea's own noise, the elderly slop and suck
Of hopeless glottals. Once, in a bad dream,
He saw himself stranded on the wet flats,
As limp as kelp, among putrescent crabs.
But to the very finish he remembered
The flash and force, the crests, the heraldry,
Those casual epergnes towering up
Like Easter trinkets of the tzarevitch.

A LOT OF NIGHT MUSIC

Even a Pyrrhonist
Who knows only that he can never know
(But adores a paradox)
Would admit it's getting dark. Pale as a wrist-
Watch numeral glow,
Fireflies build a sky among the phlox,

Imparting their faint light
Conservatively only to themselves.
Earthmurk and flowerscent
Sweeten the homes of ants. Comes on the night
When the mind rockets and delves
In blind hyperbolas of its own bent.

Above, the moon at large,
Muse-goddess, slightly polluted by the runs
Of American astronauts,
(Poor, poxed Diana, laid open to the charge
Of social Actaeons)
Mildly solicits our petty cash and thoughts.

At once with their votive mites,
Out of the woods and woodwork poets come,
Hauling their truths and booty,
Each one a Phosphor, writing by his own lights,
And with a diesel hum
Of mosquitoes or priests, proffer their wordy
duty.

They speak in tongues, no doubt;
High glossolalia, runic gibberish.
Some are like desert saints,
Wheat-germ ascetics, draped in pelt and clout.
Some come in schools, like fish.
These make their litany of dark complaints;

Those laugh and rejoice
At liberation from the bonds of gender,
Race, morals and mind,
As well as meter, rhyme and the human voice.
Still others strive to render
The cross-word world in perfectly declined

Pronouns, starting with ME.
Yet there are honest voices to be heard:
The crickets keep their vigil
Among the grass; in some invisible tree
Anonymously a bird
Whistles a fioritura, a light, vestigial

Reminder of a time,
An Aesopic Age when all the beasts were moral
And taught their ways to men;
Some herbal dream, some chlorophyll sublime
In which Apollo's laurel
Blooms in a world made innocent again.

A BIRTHDAY POEM

June 22, 1976

Like a small cloud, like a little hovering ghost
    Without substance or edges,
Like a crowd of numbered dots in a sick child's puzzle,
    A loose community of midges
Sways in the carven shafts of noon that coast
Down through the summer trees in a golden dazzle.

Intent upon such tiny copter flights,
    The eye adjusts its focus
To those billowings about ten feet away,
    That hazy, woven hocus-pocus
Or shell game of the air, whose casual sleights
Leave us unable certainly to say

What lies behind it, or what sets it off
    With fine diminishings,
Like the pale towns Mantegna chose to place
    Beyond the thieves and King of Kings:
Those domes, theatres and temples, clear enough
On that mid-afternoon of our disgrace.

And we know at once it would take an act of will
    Plus a firm, inquiring squint
To ignore those drunken motes and concentrate
    On the blurred, unfathomed background tint
Of deep sea-green Holbein employed to fill
The space behind his ministers of state,

As if one range slyly obscured the other.
    As, in the main, it does.
All of our Flemish distances disclose
    A clarity that never was:
Dwarf pilgrims in the green faubourgs of Mother
And Son, stunted cathedrals, shrunken cows.

It's the same with Time. Looked at *sub specie*
      Aeternitatis, from
The snow-line of some Ararat of years,
    Scholars remark those kingdoms come
To nothing, to grief, without the least display
Of anything so underbred as tears,

And with their Zeiss binoculars descry
      Verduns and Waterloos,
The man-made mushroom's deathly overplus,
    Caesars and heretics and Jews
Gone down in blood, without batting an eye,
As if all history were deciduous.

It's when we come to shift the gears of tense
      That suddenly we note
A curious excitement of the heart
     And slight catch in the throat:—
When, for example, from the confluence
That bears all things away I set apart

The inexpressible lineaments of your face,
      Both as I know it now,
By heart, by sight, by reverent touch and study,
     And as it once was years ago,
Back in some inaccessible time and place,
Fixed in the vanished camera of somebody.

You are four years old here in this photograph.
      You are turned out in style,
In a pair of bright red sneakers, a birthday gift.
     You are looking down at them with a smile
Of pride and admiration, half
Wonder and half joy, at the right and the left.

The picture is black and white, mere light and shade.
  Even the sneakers' red
Has washed away in acids. A voice is spent,
  Echoing down the ages in my head:
What is your substance, whereof are you made,
That millions of strange shadows on you tend?

O my most dear, I know the live imprint
  Of that smile of gratitude,
Know it more perfectly than any book.
  It brims upon the world, a mood
Of love, a mode of gladness without stint.
O that I may be worthy of that look.

RETREAT

Day peters out. Darkness wells up
    From wheelrut, culvert, vacant drain;
But still a rooster glints with life,
    High on a church's weather-vane;
The sun flings Mycenaean gold
    Against a neighbor's window-pane.

COMING HOME

From the journals of John Clare

July 18, 1841

They take away our belts so that we must hold
Our trousers up. The truly mad don't bother
And thus are oddly hobbled. Also our laces
So that our shoes do flop about our feet.
But I'm permitted exercise abroad
And feeling rather down and melancholy
Went for a forest walk. There I met gypsies
And sought their help to make good my escape
From the mad house. I confessed I had no money
But promised I should furnish them fifty pounds.
We fixed on Saturday. But when I returned
They had disappeared in their Egyptian way.
The sun set up its starlight in the trees
Which the breeze made to twinkle. They left behind
An old wide awake hat on which I battened
As it might advantage me some later time.

July 20

Calmly, as though I purposed to converse
With the birds, as I am sometimes known to do,
I walked down the lane gently and was soon
In Enfield Town and then on the great York Road
Where it was all plain sailing, where no enemy
Displayed himself and I was without fear.
I made good progress, and by the dark of night
Skirted a marsh or pond and found a hovel
Floored with thick bales of clover and laid me down
As on the harvest of a summer field,
Companion to imaginary bees.
But I was troubled by uneasy dreams.
I thought my first wife lay in my left arm

And then somebody took her from my side
Which made me wake to hear someone say, "Mary,"
But nobody was by. I was alone.

*   *   *

I've made some progress, but being without food,
It is slower now, and I must void my shoes
Of pebbles fairly often, and rest myself.
I lay in a ditch to be out of the wind's way,
Fell into sleep for half an hour or so
And waked to find the left side of me soaked
With a foul scum and a soft mantling green.

*   *   *

I travel much at night, and I remember
Walking some miles under a brilliant sky
Almost dove-grey from closely hidden moonlight
Cast on the moisture of the atmosphere
Against which the tall trees on either side
Were unimaginably black and flat
And the puddles of the road flagstones of silver.

*   *   *

On the third day, stupid with weariness
And hunger, I assuaged my appetite
With eating grass, which seemed to taste like bread,
And seemed to do me good; and once, indeed,
It satisfied a king of Babylon.
I remember passing through the town of Buckden
And must have passed others as in a trance
For I recall none till I came to Stilton
Where my poor feet gave out. I found a tussock
Where I might rest myself, and as I lay down
I heard the voice of a young woman say,

"Poor creature," and another, older voice,
"He shams," but when I rose the latter said,
"O no he don't," as I limped quickly off.
  I never saw those women, never looked back.

July 23

  I was overtaken by a man and woman
Traveling by cart, and found them to be neighbors
From Helpstone where I used to live. They saw
My ragged state and gave me alms of fivepence
By which at the public house beside the bridge
I got some bread and cheese and two half-pints
And so was much refreshed, though scarcely able
To walk, my feet being now exceeding crippled
And I required to halt more frequently,
But greatly cheered at being in home's way.
I recognized the road to Peterborough
And all my hopes were up when there came towards
    me
A cart with a man, a woman and a boy.
When they were close, the woman leaped to the
    ground,
Seized both my hands and urged me towards the cart
But I refused and thought her either drunk
Or mad, but when I was told that she was Patty,
My second wife, I suffered myself to climb
Aboard and soon arrived at Northborough.
But Mary was not there. Neither could I discover
Anything of her more than the old story
That she was six years dead, intelligence
Of a doubtful newspaper some twelve years old;
But I would not be taken in by blarney
Having seen her very self with my two eyes
About twelve months ago, alive and young
And fresh and well and beautiful as ever.

PRAISE FOR KOLONOS

Come, let us praise this haven of strong horses,
unmatched, brilliant Kolonos, white with sunlight,
where the shy one, the nightingale, at evening
      flutes in the darkness,

the ivy dark, so woven of fruit and vine-leaves
no winter storms nor light of day can enter
this sanctuary of the dancing revels
      of Dionysos.

Here, under heaven's dew, blooms the narcissus,
crown of life's mother and her buried daughter,
of Earth and the Dark below; here, too, the sunburst
      flares of the crocus.

The river's ample springs, cool and unfailing,
rove and caress this green, fair-breasted landscape.
Here have the Muses visited with dances,
      and Aphrodite

has reined her chariot here. And here is something
unheard of in the fabulous land of Asia,
unknown to Doric earth—a thing immortal;
      gift of a goddess,

beyond the control of hands, tough, self-renewing,
an enduring wealth, passing through generations,
here only: the invincible grey-leafed olive.
      Agèd survivor

of all vicissitudes, it knows protection
of the All-Seeing Eye of Zeus, whose sunlight
always regards it, and of Grey-Eyed Athena.
      I have another

tribute of praise for this city, our mother:
the greatest gift of a god, a strength of horses,
strength of young horses, a power of the ocean,
      strength and a power.

O Lord Poseidon, you have doubly blessed us
with healing skills, on these roads first bestowing
the bit that gentles horses, the controlling
      curb and the bridle,

and the carved, feathering oar that skims and dances
like the white nymphs of water, conferring mastery
of ocean roads, among the spume and wind-blown
      prancing of stallions.

From SOPHOCLES' *Oedipus at Kolonos*

SESTINA D'INVERNO

Here in this bleak city of Rochester,
Where there are twenty-seven words for "snow,"
Not all of them polite, the wayward mind
Basks in some Yucatan of its own making,
Some coppery, sleek lagoon, or cinnamon island
Alive with lemon tints and burnished natives,

And O that we were there. But here the natives
Of this grey, sunless city of Rochester
Have sown whole mines of salt about their land
(Bare ruined Carthage that it is) while snow
Comes down as if The Flood were in the making.
Yet on that ocean Marvell called the mind

An ark sets forth which is itself the mind,
Bound for some pungent green, some shore whose
    natives
Blend coriander, cayenne, mint in making
Roasts that would gladden the Earl of Rochester
With sinfulness, and melt a polar snow.
It might be well to remember that an island

Was a blessed haven once, more than an island,
The grand, utopian dream of a noble mind.
In that kind climate the mere thought of snow
Was but a wedding cake; the youthful natives,
Unable to conceive of Rochester,
Made love, and were acrobatic in the making.

Dream as we may, there is far more to making
Do than some wistful reverie of an island,
Especially now when hope lies with the Rochester
Gas and Electric Co., which doesn't mind
Such profitable weather, while the natives
Sink, like Pompeians, under a world of snow.

The one thing indisputable here is snow,
The single verity of heaven's making,
Deeply indifferent to the dreams of the natives
And the torn hoarding-posters of some island.
Under our igloo skies the frozen mind
Holds to one truth: it is grey, and called Rochester.

No island fantasy survives Rochester,
Where to the natives destiny is snow
That is neither to our mind nor of our making.

ROME

Just as foretold, it all was there.
Bone china columns gently fluted
Among the cypress groves, and the reputed
    Clarity of the air,

There was the sun-bleached skeleton
Of History with all its sins
Withered away, the slaves and citizens
    Mercifully undone.

With here and there an armature
Of iron or a wall of brick,
It lay in unhistoric peace, a trick
    Of that contrived, secure,

Arrested pterodactyl flight
Inside the museum's tank of glass;
And somehow quite unlike our Latin class
    Sepias of the site,

Discoursed upon by Mr. Fish
In the familiar, rumpled suit,
Who tried to teach us the Ablative Absolute
    And got part of his wish,

But a small part, and never traveled
On anything but the B. M. T.
Until the day of his death, when he would be,
    At length, utterly graveled.

SWAN DIVE

Over a crisp regatta of lights, or a school
Of bobbling spoons, ovals of polished black
Kiss, link, and part, wriggle and ride in place
On the lilt and rippling slide of the waterback,
And glints go skittering in a down-wind race
On smooth librations of the swimming pool,

While overhead on the tensile jut and spring
Of the highest board, a saffroned diver toes
The sisal edge, rehearsing throughout his limbs
The flight of himself, from the arching glee to the
    close
Of wet, complete acceptance, when the world dims
To nothing at all in the ear's uproar and ring.

He backs away, and then, with a loping run
And leap of released ambition, lifts to a splendid
Realm of his own, a destined place in the air,
Where, in a wash of light, he floats suspended
Above the turquoise waters, the ravelled snare
Of snaking gold, the fractured, drunken sun,

And the squints of the foreshortened girls and boys
Below in a world of envies and desires,
Eying him rise on fonts of air to sheer
And shapely grace. His dream of himself requires
A flexed attention, emptiness, a clear
Uncumbered space and sleek Daedalian poise,

From which he bows his head with abrupt assent
And sails to a perfect sacrifice below—
To a scatter of flagstone shadows, a garbled flight
Of quavering anthelions, a slow
Tumult of haloes in green, cathedral light.
Behind him trails a bright dishevelment

Of rising carbuncles of air; he sees
Light spill across the undulant mercury film
Beyond which lies his breath. And now with a
    flutter
Of fountaining arms and into a final calm
He surfaces, clutching at the tiled gutter,
Where he rides limp and smilingly at ease.

But hoisting himself out, his weight returns
To normal, like sudden aging or weariness.
Tonight, full-length on a rumpled bed, alone,
He will redream it all: bathed in success
And sweat, he will achieve the chiselled stone
Of catatonia, for which his body yearns.

"AUGURIES OF INNOCENCE"

A small, unsmiling child,
Held upon her shoulder,
Stares from a photograph
Slightly out of kilter.
It slipped from a loaded folder
Where the income tax was filed.
The light seems cut in half
By a glum, October filter.

Of course, the child is right.
The unleafed branches knot
Into hopeless riddles behind him
And the air is clearly cold.
Given the stinted light
To which fate and film consigned him,
Who'd smile at his own lot
Even at one year old?

And yet his mother smiles.
Is it grown-up make-believe,
As when anyone takes your picture
Or some nobler, Roman virtue?
Vanity? Folly? The wiles
That some have up their sleeve?
A proud and flinty stricture
Against showing that things can hurt you,

Or a dark, Medean smile?
I'd be the last to know.
A speechless child of one
Could better construe the omens,
Unriddle our gifts for guile.
There's no sign from my son.
But it needs no Greeks or Romans
To foresee the ice and snow.

PERIPETEIA

Of course, the familiar rustling of programs,
My hair mussed from behind by a grand gesture
Of mink. A little craning about to see
If anyone I know is in the audience,
And, as the house fills up,
A mild relief that no one there knows me.
A certain amount of getting up and down
From my aisle seat to let the others in.
Then my eyes wander briefly over the cast,
Management, stand-ins, make-up men, designers,
Perfume and liquor ads, and rise prayerlike
To the false heaven of rosetted lights,
The stucco lyres and emblems of high art
That promise, with crude Broadway honesty,
Something less than perfection:
Two bulbs are missing and Apollo's bored.

And then the cool, drawn-out anticipation,
Not of the play itself, but the false dusk
And equally false night when the houselights
Obey some planetary rheostat
And bring a stillness on. It is that stillness
I wait for.
                    Before it comes,
Whether we like it or not, we are a crowd,
Foul-breathed, gum-chewing, fat with arrogance,
Passion, opinion, and appetite for blood.
But in that instant, which the mind protracts,
From dim to dark before the curtain rises,
Each of us is miraculously alone
In calm, invulnerable isolation,
Neither a neighbor nor a fellow but,
As at the beginning and end, a single soul,
With all the sweet and sour of loneliness.
I, as a connoisseur of loneliness,

Savor it richly, and set it down
In an endless umber landscape, a stubble field
Under a lilac, electric, storm-flushed sky,
Where, in companionship with worthless stones,
Mica-flecked, or at best some rusty quartz,
I stood in childhood, waiting for things to mend.
A useful discipline, perhaps. One that might lead
To solitary, self-denying work
That issues in something harmless, like a poem,
Governed by laws that stand for other laws,
Both of which aim, through kindred disciplines,
At the soul's knowledge and habiliment.
In any case, in a self-granted freedom,
The mind, lone regent of itself, prolongs
The dark and silence; mirrors itself, delights
In consciousness of consciousness, alone,
Sufficient, nimble, touched with a small grace.

Then, as it must at last, the curtain rises,
The play begins. Something by Shakespeare.
Framed in the arched proscenium, it seems
A dream, neither better nor worse
Than whatever I shall dream after I rise
With hat and coat, go home to bed, and dream.
If anything, more limited, more strict—
No one will fly or turn into a moose.
But acceptable, like a dream, because remote,
And there is, after all, a pretty girl.
Perhaps tonight she'll figure in the cast
I summon to my slumber and control
In vast arenas, limitless space, and time
That yield and sway in soft Einsteinian tides.
Who is she? Sylvia? Amelia Earhart?
Some creature that appears and disappears
From life, from reverie, a fugitive of dreams?
There on the stage, with awkward grace, the actors,
Beautifully costumed in Renaissance brocade,

141

Perform their duties, even as I must mine,
Though not, as I am, always free to smile.

Something is happening. Some consternation.
Are the knives out? Is someone's life in danger?
And can the magic cloak and book protect?
One has, of course, real confidence in Shakespeare.
And I relax in my plush seat, convinced
That prompt as dawn and genuine as a toothache
The dream will be accomplished, provisionally true
As anything else one cares to think about.
The players are aghast. Can it be the villain,
The outrageous drunks, plotting the coup d'état,
Are slyer than we thought? Or we more innocent?
Can it be that poems lie? As in a dream,
Leaving a stunned and gap-mouthed Ferdinand,
Father and faery pageant, she, even she,
Miraculous Miranda, steps from the stage,
Moves up the aisle to my seat, where she stops,
Smiles gently, seriously, and takes my hand
And leads me out of the theatre, into a night
As luminous as noon, more deeply real,
Simply because of her hand, than any dream
Shakespeare or I or anyone ever dreamed.

AFTER THE RAIN

for W. D. Snodgrass

The barbed-wire fences rust
As their cedar uprights blacken
After a night of rain.
Some early, innocent lust
Gets me outdoors to smell
The teasle, the pelted bracken,
The cold, mossed-over well,
Rank with its iron chain,

And takes me off for a stroll.
Wetness has taken over.
From drain and creeper twine
It's runnelled and trenched and edged
A pebbled serpentine
Secretly, as though pledged
To attain a difficult goal
And join some important river.

The air is a smear of ashes
With a cool taste of coins.
Stiff among misty washes,
The trees are as black as wicks,
Silent, detached and old.
A pallor undermines
Some damp and swollen sticks.
The woods are rich with mould.

How even and pure this light!
All things stand on their own,
Equal and shadowless,
In a world gone pale and neuter,
Yet riddled with fresh delight.
The heart of every stone
Conceals a toad, and the grass
Shines with a douse of pewter.

Somewhere a branch rustles
With the life of squirrels or birds,
Some life that is quick and right.
This queer, delicious bareness,
This plain, uniform light,
In which both elms and thistles,
Grass, boulders, even words,
Speak for a Spartan fairness,

Might, as I think it over,
Speak in a form of signs,
If only one could know
All of its hidden tricks,
Saying that I must go
With a cool taste of coins
To join some important river,
Some damp and swollen Styx.

Yet what puzzles me the most
Is my unwavering taste
For these dim, weathery ghosts,
And how, from the very first,
An early, innocent lust
Delighted in such wastes,
Sought with a reckless thirst
A light so pure and just.

APPLES FOR PAUL SUTTMAN

Chardin, Cézanne, they had their apples,
    As did Paris and Eve—
Sleek, buxom pippins with inverted nipples;
    And surely we believe

That Pluto has his own unsweet earth apples
    Blooming among the dead,
There in the thick of Radamanthine opals,
    Blake's hand, Bernini's head.

Ours are not golden overtures to trouble
    Or molds of fatal choice,
But like some fleshed epitome, the apple
    Entreats us to rejoice

In more than flavor, nourishment, or color,
    Or jack or calvados;
Nor are we rendered, through ingested dolor,
    Sinful or comatose.

It speaks to us quite otherwise, in supple
    Convexity and ply,
Smooth, modeled slopes, familiar rills. Crab apple,
    Winesap and Northern Spy

Tell us Hogarth's "Analysis of Beauty"
    Or architect's French Curve
Cannot proclaim what Aphrodite's putti
    Both celebrate and serve:

Those known hyperbolas, those rounds and
        gradients,
    Dingle and shadowed dip,
The commonwealth of joy, imagined radiance,
    Thoughts of that faultless lip.

> The dearest curves in nature—the merest ripple,
>   The cresting wave—release
> All of our love, and find it in an apple,
>   My Helen, your Elisse.

THE HUNT

for Zbigniew Herbert

I

A call, a call. Ringbolt clinks at dusk. Shadows wax. Sesame.
Here are earthworms, and the dry needles of pine. I am
hidden. Gems in their harness might be stars, picked out.
Lovely to see, trust me. And the stone is protection,wouldn't
you say? This is my stone, gentle as snow, trust me. Darkness helps. Let us eat. The air, promise-crammed. And so
the poor dog had none. I saw three in sunlight. One had a
pearwood bow, like Cupid's upper lip. I whisper my love to
this rock. I have always loved it. Sesame. A caul, a caul.
Where is Lady Luck in the forest? Well, there's no moon.
Once I had apples. Let us pray. They have great weight,
the bronze fittings of Magyar kings. Their trumpets are
muted. But the tall trees gather here, friendly. What is that
fluttering, there? I can't make out. All the dark sweet dens
of the foxes are full of stink and safety. That was a tasty one.
Just to go down, there with pale roots and hidden waters.
O hidden. Is anyone hungry? He laughed, you know, and
shook my hand. I must not say that. O the dear stone. Owls
are out; mice, take warning. All those little squeaks must
be death-cries. You're welcome. Trust me, trust me. But
didn't he laugh? So help me.

I I

I am much too tired now to do anything
But look at the molding along the top of the wall.
Those orchid shadows and pearl highlights bring
My childhood back so oddly. They recall

Two weeks of scarlet fever, when I lay
Gazing at grooves and bevels, oyster whites
Clouding to ringdove feathers, gathering lights
Like snow on railings towards the middle of day.

Just to lie there and watch, astonished when
That subtle show gave way to electric light,
That's what I think of, lying here tonight.
Tonight the interrogations begin again.

EXILE

for Joseph Brodsky

Vacant parade grounds swept by the winter wind,
A pile of worn-out tires crowning a knoll,
The purplish clinkers near the cinder blocks
That support the steps of an abandoned church
Still moored to a telephone pole, this sullen place
Is *terra deserta*, Joseph, this is Egypt.

You have been here before, but long ago.
The first time you were sold by your own brothers
But had a gift for dreams that somehow saved you.
The second time was familiar but still harder.
You came with wife and child, the child not yours,
The wife, whom you adored, in a way not yours,
And all that you can recall, even in dreams,
Is the birth itself, and after that the journey,
Mixed with an obscure and confusing music,
Confused with a smell of hay and steaming dung.
Nothing is clear from then on, and what became
Of the woman and child eludes you altogether.

Look, though, at the blank, expressionless faces
Here in this photograph by Walker Evans.
These are the faces that everywhere surround you;
They have all the emptiness of gravel pits.
And look, here, at this heavy growth of weeds
Where the dishwater is poured from the kitchen
    window
And has been ever since the house was built.
And the chimney whispers its weak diphtheria,
The hydrangeas display their gritty pollen of soot.
This is Egypt, Joseph, the old school of the soul.
You will recognize the rank smell of a stable
And the soft patience in a donkey's eyes,
Telling you you are welcome and at home.

THE FEAST OF STEPHEN

The coltish horseplay of the locker room,
Moist with the steam of the tiled shower stalls,
With shameless blends of civet, musk and sweat,
Loud with the cap-gun snapping of wet towels
Under the steel-ribbed cages of bare bulbs,
In some such setting of thick basement pipes
And janitorial realities
Boys for the first time frankly eye each other,
Inspect each others' bodies at close range,
And what they see is not so much another
As a strange, possible version of themselves,
And all the sparring dance, adrenal life,
Tense, jubilant nimbleness, is but a vague,
Busy, unfocused ballet of self-love.

II

If the heart has its reasons, perhaps the body
Has its own lumbering sort of carnal spirit,
Felt in the tingling bruises of collision,
And known to captains as *esprit de corps*.
What is this brisk fraternity of timing,
Pivot and lobbing arc, or indirection,
Mens sana in men's sauna, in the flush
Of health and toilets, private and corporal glee,
These fleet caroms, *pliés* and genuflections
Before the salmon-leap, the leaping fountain
All sheathed in glistening light, flexed and alert?
From the vast echo-chamber of the gym,
Among the scumbled shouts and shrill of whistles,
The bounced basketball sound of a leather whip.

III

Think of those barren places where men gather
To act in the terrible name of rectitude,
Of acned shame, punk's pride, muscle or turf,
The bully's thin superiority.
Think of the *Sturm-Abteilungs Kommandant*
Who loves Beethoven and collects Degas,
Or the blond boys in jeans whose narrowed eyes
Are focussed by some hard and smothered lust,
Who lounge in a studied mimicry of ease,
Flick their live butts into the standing weeds,
And comb their hair in the mirror of cracked
     windows
Of an abandoned warehouse where they keep
In darkened readiness for their occasion
The rope, the chains, handcuffs and gasoline.

IV

Out in the rippled heat of a neighbor's field,
In the kilowatts of noon, they've got one cornered.
The bugs are jumping, and the burly youths
Strip to the waist for the hot work ahead.
They go to arm themselves at the dry-stone wall,
Having flung down their wet and salty garments
At the feet of a young man whose name is Saul.
He watches sharply these superbly tanned
Figures with a swimmer's chest and shoulders,
A miler's thighs, with their self-conscious grace,
And in between their sleek, converging bodies,
Brilliantly oiled and burnished by the sun,
He catches a brief glimpse of bloodied hair
And hears an unintelligible prayer.

THE ODDS

for Evan

Three new and matching loaves,
Each set upon a motionless swing seat,
Straight from some elemental stoves
And winter bakeries of unearthly wheat,
In diamonded, smooth pillowings of white
Have risen out of nothing overnight.

And all the woods for miles,
Stooped by these clean endowments of the north,
Flaunt the same candle-dripping styles
In poured combers of pumice and the froth
Of heady steins. Upon the railings lodge
The fat shapes of a nineteen-thirties Dodge.

Such perilous, toppling tides;
Such teeterings along uncertain perches.
A fragile cantilever hides
Even the chevrons of our veteran birches.
In this fierce hush there is a spell that heaves
Those huge arrested oceans in the eaves.

A sort of stagy show
Put on by a spoiled, eccentric millionaire.
Lacking the craft and choice that go
With weighed precision, meditated care,
Into a work of art, these are the spent,
Loose, aimless squanderings of the discontent.

Like the blind, headlong cells,
Crowding toward dreams of life, only to die
In dark fallopian canals,
Or that wild strew of bodies at My Lai.
Thick drifts, huddled embankments at our door
Pile up in this eleventh year of war.

Yet to these April snows,
This rashness, those incalculable odds,
The costly and cold-blooded shows
Of blind perversity or spendthrift gods
My son is born, and in his mother's eyes
Turns the whole war and winter into lies.

But voices underground
Demand, "Who died for him? Who gave him
place?"
I have no answer. Vaguely stunned,
I turn away and look at my wife's face.
Outside the simple miracle of this birth
The snowflakes lift and swivel to the earth

As in those crystal balls
With Christmas storms of manageable size,
A chalk precipitate that shawls
Antlers and roof and gifts beyond surmise,
A tiny settlement among those powers
That shape our world, but that are never ours.

APPREHENSIONS

A grave and secret malady of my brother's,
The stock exchange, various grown-up shames,
The white emergency of hospitals,
Inquiries from the press, such *coups de théâtre*
Upon a stage from which I was excluded
Under the rubric of "benign neglect"
Had left me pretty much to my own devices
(My own stage was about seven years old)
Except for a Teutonic governess
Replete with the curious thumb-print of her race,
That special relish for inflicted pain.
Some of this she could vaguely satisfy
In the pages of the *Journal-American*
Which featured stories with lurid photographs—
A child chained tightly to a radiator
In an abandoned house; the instruments
With which some man tortured his fiancée,
A headless body recently unearthed
On the links of an exclusive country club—
That fleshed out terribly what loyal readers
Hankered for daily in the name of news.
(It in no way resembled the *New York Times*,
My parents' paper, thin on photographs.)
Its world, some half-lit world, some demi-monde,
I knew of only through Fräulein's addiction
To news that was largely terminal and obscene,
Winding its way between the ads for nightclubs
With girls wearing top hats, black tie, wing collar,
But without shirts, their naked breasts exposed;
And liquids that removed unsightly hair,
Treatments for corns, trusses and belts and braces.
She chain-smoked Camels as she scanned the pages,
Whereas my mother's brand was Chesterfield.

My primary education was composed
Of daily lessons in placating her
With acts of shameless, mute docility.
At seven I knew that I was not her equal,
If I knew nothing else. And I knew little,
But suspected a great deal—domestic quarrels,
Not altogether muffled, must have meant something.
"The market" of our home was the stock market,
Without visible fruit, without produce,
Except perhaps for the strange vendors of apples
Who filled our city streets. And all those girls—
The ones with naked breasts—there was some secret,
Deep as my brother's illness, behind their smiles.
They knew something I didn't; they taunted me.
I moved in a cloudy world of inference
Where the most solid object was a toy
Rake that my governess had used to beat me.

My own devices came to silence and cunning
In my unwilling exile, while attempting
To put two and two together, at which I failed.
The world seemed made of violent oppositions:
The Bull and Bear of Wall Street, Mother and Father,
Criminals and their victims, Venus and Mars,
The cold, portending graphics of the stars.
I spent my time in what these days my son
At three years old calls "grabbling around,"
For which Roget might possibly supply
"Purposeful idling, staying out of the way,"
Or, in the military phrase, "gold-bricking,"
A serious occupation, for which I was gifted
One Christmas with an all but magic treasure:
The Book of Knowledge, complete in twenty volumes.
I was its refugee, it was my Forest
Stocked with demure princesses, tameable dragons,
And sway-backed cottages, weighted with snow,
And waiting in an Arthur Rackham mist

For the high, secret advent of Santa Claus.
Dim populations of elfdom, and what's more,
Pictures of laborers in derby hats
And shirtsleeves, Thomas Alva Edison,
Who seemed to resemble Harding, who, in turn,
Resembled a kindly courtier, tactfully whispering
In the ear of Isabella, Queen of Spain—
Probably bearing on financial matters,
Selling the family jewels for Columbus,
Or whether the world is round. Serious topics
To which I would give due consideration.
There were puzzles and, magnificently, their answers;
Lively depictions of the Trojan War;
And Mrs. Siddons as The Tragic Muse.
Methods of calculating the height of trees,
Maps of the earth and heavens, buccaneer
Ventures for buried gold, and poetry:
Whittier, Longfellow, and "Home, Sweet Home."
Here was God's plenty, as Dryden said of Chaucer.

Inestimable, priceless as that gift was,
I was given yet another—more peculiar,
Rare, unexpected, harder to assess,
An experience that W. H. Auden
Designates as "The Vision of Dame Kind,"
Remarking that "the objects of this vision
May be inorganic—mountains, rivers, seas,—
Or organic—trees and beasts—but they're non-human,
Though human artifacts may be included."

We were living at this time in New York City
On the sixth floor of an apartment house
On Lexington, which still had streetcar tracks.
It was an afternoon in the late summer;
The windows open; wrought-iron window guards
Meant to keep pets and children from falling out.
I, at the window, studiously watching

A marvelous transformation of the sky;
A storm was coming up by dark gradations.
But what was curious about this was
That as the sky seemed to be taking on
An ashy blankness, behind which there lay
Tonalities of lilac and dusty rose
Tarnishing now to something more than dusk,
Crepuscular and funerary greys,
The streets became more luminous, the world
Glinted and shone with an uncanny freshness.
The brickwork of the house across the street
(A grim, run-down Victorian chateau)
Became distinct and legible; the air,
Full of excited imminence, stood still.
The streetcar tracks gleamed like the path of snails.
And all of this made me superbly happy,
But most of all a yellow Checker Cab
Parked at the corner. Something in the light
Was making this the yellowest thing on earth.
It was as if Adam, having completed
Naming the animals, had started in
On colors, and had found his primary pigment
Here, in a taxi cab, on Eighty-ninth street.
It was the absolute, parental yellow.
Trash littered the gutter, the chipped paint
Of the lamppost still was chipped, but everything
Seemed meant to be as it was, seemed so designed,
As if the world had just then been created,
Not as a garden, but a rather soiled,
Loud, urban intersection, by God's will.
And then a chart of the Mississippi River,
With all her tributaries, flashed in the sky.
Thunder, beginning softly and far away,
Rolled down our avenue towards an explosion
That started with the sound of ripping cloth
And ended with a crash that made all crashes
Feeble, inadequate preliminaries.

And it began to rain. Someone or other
Called me away from there, and closed the window.

Reverberations (from the Latin, *verber*,
Meaning a whip or lash) rang down the alley
Of Lower Manhattan where George Washington
Stood in the cold, eying the ticker-tape,
Its latest bulletins getting worse and worse,
A ticking code of terminal messages.
The family jewels were gone. What had Columbus
(Who looked so noble in The Book of Knowledge)
Found for himself? Leg-irons. The Jersey flats.
More bodies than the *Journal-American*
Could well keep count of, most of them Indians.
And then one day there was discovered missing
My brother's bottle of phenobarbitol—
And, as it later turned out, a razor blade.
How late in coming were all the revelations.
How dark and Cabbalistic the mysteries.
Messages all in cipher, enthymemes
Grossly suggestive, keeping their own counsel,
Vivid and unintelligible dreams.
A heartless regimen of exercises
Performed upon a sort of doorway gym
Was meant to strengthen my brother's hand and arm,
As hours with a stereopticon
His eyesight. But the doctor's tactful whispers
Were sibilant, Sibylline, inaudible.
There were, at last, when he returned to us,
My father's bandaged wrists. All the elisions
Cried loudly in a tongue I didn't know.
Finally, in the flat, declarative sentence
Of the encephalograph, the news was in:
In shocking lines the instrument described
My brother's malady as what the French,
Simply and full of awe, call *"le grand mal,"*
The Great Disease, Caesar's and Dostoievski's.

All of this seemed to prove, in a world where proof
Was often stinting, and the clues ominous,
That the *Journal-American* after all was right:
That sex was somehow wedded to disaster,
Pleasure and pain were necessary twins,
And that The Book of Knowledge and my vision
(Or whatever it was) were to be put away
With childish things, as, in the end, the world
As well as holy text insist upon.

     Just when it was that Fräulein disappeared
I don't recall. We continued to meet each other
By secret assignations in my dreams
In which, by stages, our relationship
Grew into international proportions
As the ghettos of Europe emptied, the box cars
Rolled toward enclosures terminal and obscene,
The ovens blazed away like Pittsburgh steel mills,
Chain-smoking through the night, and no one spoke.
We two would meet in a darkened living room
Between the lines of advancing allied troops
In the Wagnerian twilight of the *Reich*.
She would be seated by a table, reading
Under a lamp-shade of the finest parchment.
She would look up and say, "I always knew
That you would come to me, that you'd come home."
I would read over her shoulder, *"In der Heimat,
Im Heimatland, da gibts ein Wiedersehen."*
An old song of comparative innocence,
Until one learns to read between the lines.

THE GHOST IN THE MARTINI

Over the rim of the glass
Containing a good martini with a twist
I eye her bosom and consider a pass,
Certain we'd not be missed

In the general hubbub.
Her lips, which I forgot to say, are superb,
Never stop babbling once (Aye, there's the rub)
But who would want to curb

Such delicious, artful flattery?
It seems she adores my work, the distinguished
grey
Of my hair. I muse on the salt and battery
Of the sexual clinch, and say

Something terse and gruff
About the marked disparity in our ages.
She looks like twenty-three, though eager enough.
As for the famous wages

Of sin, she can't have attained
Even to union scale, though you never can tell.
Her waist is slender and suggestively chained,
And things are going well.

The martini does its job,
God bless it, seeping down to the dark old id.
("Is there no cradle, Sir, you would not rob?"
Says ego, but the lid

Is off. The word is Strike
While the iron's hot.) And now, ingenuous and
gay,
She is asking me about what I was like
At twenty. (Twenty, eh?)

You wouldn't have liked me then,
I answer, looking carefully into her eyes.
I was shy, withdrawn, awkward, one of those men
    That girls seemed to despise,

Moody and self-obsessed,
Unhappy, defiant, with guilty dreams galore,
Full of ill-natured pride, an unconfessed
    Snob and a thorough bore.

Her smile is meant to convey
How changed or modest I am, I can't tell which,
When I suddenly hear someone close to me say,
    "You lousy son-of-a-bitch!"

A young man's voice, by the sound,
Coming, it seems, from the twist in the martini.
"You arrogant, elderly letch, you broken-down
    Brother of Apeneck Sweeney!

Thought I was buried for good
Under six thick feet of mindless self-regard?
Dance on my grave, would you, you galliard stud,
    Silenus in leotard?

Well, summon me you did,
And I come unwillingly, like Samuel's ghost.
'All things shall be revealed that have been hid.'
    There's something for you to toast!

You only got where you are
By standing upon my ectoplasmic shoulders,
And wherever that is may not be so high or far
    In the eyes of some beholders.

Take, for example, me.
I have sat alone in the dark, accomplishing little,
And worth no more to myself, in pride and fee,
Than a cup of luke-warm spittle.

But honest about it, withal. . ."
("Withal," forsooth!) "Please not to interrupt.
And the lovelies went by, 'the long and the short
and the tall,'
Hankered for, but untupped.

Bloody monastic it was.
A neurotic mixture of self-denial and fear;
The verse halting, the cataleptic pause,
No sensible pain, no tear,

But an interior drip
As from an ulcer, where, in the humid deep
Center of myself, I would scratch and grip
The wet walls of the keep,

Or lie on my back and smell
From the corners the sharp, ammoniac, urine
stink.
'*No light, but rather darkness visible.*'
And plenty of time to think.

In that thick, fetid air
I talked to myself in giddy recitative:
'*I have been studying how I may compare
This prison where I live*

Unto the world. . .' I learned
Little, and was awarded no degrees.
Yet all that sunken hideousness earned
Your negligence and ease.

Nor was it wholly sick,
Having procured you a certain modest fame;
A devotion, rather, a grim device to stick
    To something I could not name."

Meanwhile, she babbles on
About men, or whatever, and the juniper juice
Shuts up at last, having sung, I trust, like a swan.
    Still given to self-abuse!

Better get out of here;
If he opens his trap again it could get much worse.
I touch her elbow, and, leaning toward her ear,
    Tell her to find her purse.

GOING THE ROUNDS:
A SORT OF LOVE POEM

Some people cannot endure
Looking down from the parapet atop the Empire State
Or the Statue of Liberty—they go limp, insecure,
The vertiginous height hums to their numbered bones
Some homily on Fate;
Neither virtue past nor vow to be good atones

To the queasy stomach, the quick,
Involuntary softening of the bowels.
"What goes up must come down," it hums: the
ultimate, sick
Joke of Fortuna. The spine, the world vibrates
With terse, ruthless avowals
From "The Life of More," "A Mirror For Magistrates."

And there are heights of spirit.
And one of these is love. From way up here,
I observe the puny view, without much merit,
Of all my days. High on the house are nailed
Banners of pride and fear.
And that small wood to the west, the girls I have failed.

It is, on the whole, rather glum:
The cyclone fence, the tar-stained railroad ties,
With, now and again, surprising the viewer, some
Garden of selflessness or effort. And, as I must,
I acknowledge on this high rise
The ancient metaphysical distrust.

But candor is not enough,
Nor is it enough to say that I don't deserve
Your gentle, dazzling love, or to be in love.
That goddess is remorseless, watching us rise
        In all our ignorant nerve,
And when we have reached the top, putting us wise.

        My dear, in spite of this,
And the moralized landscape down there below,
Neither of which might seem the ground for bliss,
Know that I love you, know that you are most dear
        To one who seeks to know
How, for your sake, to confront his pride and fear.

I I

No sooner have the words got past my lips—
        (I exaggerate for effect)
But two months later you have packed your grips
And left. And left eye-shadow, Kotex, bra,
A blue silk slip-dress that I helped select,
        And Fortuna shouts, "Hurrah!

Who does that crazy bastard think he is?
        I'll fix his wagon!"
As indeed she has. Or, as Shakespeare puts it, "''Tis
Brief, my lord.' 'As woman's love.'" He knew,
Though our arch-scholiast of the spirit's agon,
        Nothing, of course, of you.

And what am I to say? "Well, at least it will do
        For a poem."? From way down here,
The Guy in the Lake, I gaze at the distant blue
Beyond the surface, and twice as far away.
Deep in the mirror, I am reversed but clear.
        And what am I to say?

Sackville would smile. Well, let him smile. To say
      Nothing about those girls
I turned into wood, like Daphne. And every day
Cavendish mutters about his Cardinal, scorned
Son-of-a-butcher. More God damn moral pearls.
      Well, I had been warned.

Yet when I dream, it's more than of your hair,
      Your privates, voice, or face;
These deeps remind me we are still not square.
A fog thickens into cold smoke. Perhaps
You too will remember the terror of that place,
      The breakers' dead collapse,

The cry of the boy, pulled out by the undertow,
      Growing dimmer and more wild,
And how, the dark currents sucking from below,
When I was not your lover or you my wife,
Yourself exhausted and six months big with child,
      You saved my son's life.

GOLIARDIC SONG

In classical environs
    Deity misbehaves;
There nereids and sirens
    Bucket the whomping waves.
As tritons sound their conches
    With fat, distended cheeks,
Welded are buxom haunches
    To muscular physiques.

Out of that frothy pageant
    Venus Pandemos rose,
Great genetrix and regent
    Of human unrepose.
Not age nor custom cripples
    Her strenuous commands,
Imperative of nipples
    And tyrannous of glands.

We who have been her students,
    Matriculated clerks
In scholia of imprudence
    And vast, venereal Works,
Taken and passed our orals,
    Salute her classic poise:
Ur-Satirist of Morals
    And Mother of our Joys.

"GLADNESS OF THE BEST"

for Hays Rockwell

Let us get up early to the vineyards; let us
see if the vine flourish, whether the tender
grape appear, and the pomegranates bud forth:
there will I give thee my loves.

See, see upon a field of royal blue,
Scaling the steep escarpments of the sky
      With gold-leafed curlicue,
Sepals and plumula and filigree,
      This vast, untrellised vine
Of scroll- and fretwork, a Jesse's family tree
Or ivy whose thick clamberings entwine
Heaven and earth and the viewer's raddling eye.

This mealed and sprinkled glittering, this park
Of 'flowres delice' and Gobelin *millefleurs*
      Coiling upon the dark
In wild tourbillions, gerbs and golden falls
      Is a mere lace or grille
Before which Jesus works his miracles
Of love, feeding the poor, curing the ill,
Here in the Duc de Berry's *Très Riches Heures*;

And is itself the visible counterpart
Of fugal consort, branched polyphony,
      That dense, embroidered art
Of interleaved and deftly braided song
      In which each separate voice
Seems to discover where it should belong
Among its kind, and, fated by its choice,
Pursues a purpose at once fixed and free;

And every *cantus*, firm in its own pursuits,
Fluent and yet cast, as it were, in bronze,
      Exchanges brief salutes
And bows of courtesy at every turn
      With every neighboring friend,
Bends to oblige each one with quick concern
And join them at a predetermined end
Of cordial and confirming antiphons.

Such music in its turn becomes the trope
Or figure of that holy amity
      Which is our only hope,
Enjoined upon us from two mountain heights:
      On Tables of The Law
Given at Sinai, and the Nazarite's
Luminous sermon that reduced to awe
And silence a vast crowd near Galilee.

Who could have known this better than St. George,
The Poet, in whose work these things are woven
      Or wrought as at a forge
Of disappointed hopes, of triumphs won
      Through strains of sound and soul
In that small country church at Bemerton?
This was the man who styled his ghostly role,
"Domestic servant to the King of Heaven."

If then, as in the counterpoises of
Music, the laity may bless the priest
      In an exchange of love,
Riposta for *Proposta*, all we inherit
      Returned and newly named
In the established words, "and with thy spirit,"
Be it with such clear grace as his who claimed,
Of all God's mercies, he was less than least.

POEM UPON THE LISBON DISASTER

Or, An Inquiry Into The Adage, "All Is For The Best."

Woeful mankind, born to a woeful earth!
Feeble humanity, whole hosts from birth
Eternally, purposelessly distressed!
Those savants erred who claim, "All's for the best."
Approach and view this carnage, broken stone,
Rags, rubble, chips of shattered wood and bone,
Women and children pinioned under beams,
Crushed under stones, piled under severed limbs;
These hundred thousands whom the earth devours,
Cut down to bleed away their final hours.
In answer to the frail, half-uttered cry,
The smoking ashes, will you make reply,
"God, in His bounty, urged by a just cause,
Herein exhibits His eternal laws"?
Seeing these stacks of victims, will you state,
"Vengence is God's; they have deserved their fate"?
What crimes were done, what evils manifest,
By babes who died while feeding at the breast?
Did wiped-out Lisbon's sins so much outweigh
Paris and London's, who keep holiday?
Lisbon is gone, yet Paris drinks champagne.
O tranquil minds who contemplate the pain
And shipwreck of your brothers' battered forms,
And, housed in peace, debate the cause of storms,
When once you feel Fate's catalogue of woe,
Tears and humanity will start and show.
When earth gapes for me while I'm sound and
    whole
My cries will issue from the very soul.
Hemmed in by Fate's grotesque brutalities,
Wrath of the wicked, death-traps and disease,
Tried by the warring elements, we have borne
Suffering enough to sorrow and to mourn.
You claim it's pride, the first sin of the race,
That human beings, having fallen from grace,

Dream of evading Justice's decree
By means of Man's Perfectibility.
Go ask the Tagus river banks, go pry
Among the smouldering alleyways where lie
The slowly perishing, and inquire today
Whether it's simply pride that makes them pray,
"O heaven save me, heaven pity me."
"All's Good," you claim, "and all's Necessity."
Without this gulf, would the whole universe,
Still stained with Lisbon, be that much the worse?
And has the Great Creative Power no way
To teach us but by violence and decay?
Would you thus limit God? Or claim His powers
Do not extend to these concerns of ours?
I beg our Maker, humbly, from the heart,
That this brimstone catastrophe depart,
Spend its fierce heat in some far desert place.
God I respect; poor mortals I embrace.
When, scourged like this, men venture to complain,
It is not pride that speaks, it is felt pain.
     Would it console those sufferers galore,
Tormented natives of that desolate shore,
If someone said, "Drop dead with peace of mind;
Your homes were smashed for the good of human-
          kind;
And they shall be rebuilt by others' craft,
Who shall inhabit where once you lived and
          laughed.
The North shall profit by your vast demise,
And by astute investment realize
Your momentary loss and fatal pain
Conduced, through general laws, to ultimate gain.
To the far eye of God you are as base
As worms that dine and crawl upon your face"?
This were to heap some last, insulting stones
Of language on that monument of groans.

Do not presume to soothe such misery
With the fixed laws of calm necessity,
With The Great Chain of Being, hymned by Pope.
O dream of sages! O phantasmal hope!
That chain depends from God, Who is unchained;
By His beneficent will all is ordained;
He is unshackled, tractable, and just.
How comes He, then, to violate our trust?
There's the strange knot that needs to be untied!
Anguish cannot be cured by being denied.
All men, in fear of God, have sought the root
Of evil, whose mere existence you dispute.
If He, Whose hands all motions can contain,
Can launch a landslide with a hurricane
And split great oaks with lightning at a glance,
They harbor no regrets at the mischance;
But I, who live and feel in wracked dismay,
Yearn for His aid Who made me out of clay.

Children of the Almighty, born to grief,
Beseech their common Father for relief.
The potter is not questioned by the pot:
"Why is my substance dull, why frail my lot?"
It lacks capacity for speech and thought.
And yet this pot, fractured when newly wrought,
Was not, we know, provided with a heart
To wish for good or feel misfortune's smart.
"Our woe," you say, "is someone else's weal."
My body must supply the maggot's meal.
O the sweet solace of my heaped-up woes:
To be the nest of worms in my repose!
O bitter calculus of averaged grief
That adds to sorrow, offers no relief.
This is the impotent effort of the proud:
To posit joys that they are not allowed.

I'm but a small part of the Master Plan,
True, but all beings sentenced to life's span,
All sentient creatures, as the statute saith,

Must ache through life, and end, like me, in death.
    The bloody-taloned vulture in his day
Devours with joy the dead meat of his prey,
And all seems well with him; but soon he must
Bow to the eagle's beak, and bite the dust.
Man wings the haughty eagle with a shot;
And when at length it comes Man's turn to rot
Upon a battlefield, he becomes the swill
On which the birds, triumphant, eat their fill.
Thus are all creatures brother unto brother,
The heirs of pain, the death of one another.
And you would cull, in such chaos as this,
From individual miseries, general bliss.
What bliss! Yet weak and troubled you declare,
"All's for the best," in accents of despair;
The universe refutes you, and your pulse
Inwardly knows the argument is false.
    Men, beasts, and atoms, all is war and strife;
Here upon earth, be it granted, evil's rife,
Its origin beyond our powers to guess.
Could it proceed from God's high blessedness?
Or does Greek Typhon, Persian Ahriman
Condemn to woes the ground we tread upon?
I reject such brute embodiments of fear,
Those deities of a craven yesteryear.
    But how conceive the Essence of all Good,
Source of all Joys and Love, pure Fatherhood,
Swamping His little ones in storms of ill?
How could we plumb the depth of such a Will?
From Flawless Love ills can have no descent;
Nor from elsewhere, since God's omnipotent;
Yet they exist. Such paradox has checked
And baffled the weak human intellect.
A God once came to assuage our suffering,
Visited earth, but didn't change a thing!
One sophist claims He couldn't; in reply
Another says He could but didn't try,

Yet, someday, shall—and while they ergotize
Earth splits apart and all of Lisbon dies,
And thirty cities are levelled and laid plane
From the Tagus to the southern tip of Spain.
    Either God chastens Man, instinct with sin,
Or else this Lord of Space and Suserain
Of Being, indifferent, tranquil, pitiless,
Drowns us in oecumenical distress.
Either crude matter, counter to God's laws,
Bears in itself its *necessary* flaws,
Or else God tests and troubles us that we
May pass these straits into eternity.
We cancel here our fleeting host of woes:
Death is their end, our good, and our repose.
But though we end the trials we have been given
Who can lay claim upon the joys of heaven?
    Whatever ground one takes is insecure:
There's nothing we may not fear, or know for sure.
Put to the rack, Nature is stubbornly mute,
And in men's language God will not dispute.
It behooves Him nothing to explain His ways,
Console the feeble, or instruct the wise.
Yet without God, a prey to trick and doubt,
Man grasps at broken reeds to help him out.
Leibnitz cannot explain what bonds coerce,
In this best-possible-ordered universe,
Mixtures of chaos ever to destroy
With thorns of pain our insubstantial joy;
Nor why both wicked men and innocent
Sustain alike a destined punishment.
How shall this best of orders come to be?
I am all ignorance, like a Ph.D.
    Plato declares that mankind once had wings,
And flesh invulnerable to mortal stings.
No grief, no death accomplished his dismay.
How fallen from that state is his today!
He cringes, suffers, dies, like all things born;

Wherever Nature rules, her subjects mourn.
A thin pastiche of nerves and ligaments
Can't rise above the warring elements;
This recipe of dust, bones, spirits and blood,
No sooner mixed, dissolves itself for good.
Those nerves respond especially to gloom,
Sorrow and dark, harbingers of the tomb.
There speaks the voice of Nature, and negates
Plato's and Epicurus' postulates.
Pierre Bayle knew more than both: I'll seek him
    out.
With scales in hand, under the flag of Doubt,
Rejecting all closed systems by sheer strength
Of mind and command of stature, Bayle at length
Has overthrown all systems, overthrown
Even those bleak constructions of his own;
Like that blind hero, powerful in his chains,
Self-immolated with the Philistines.
    What may the most exalted spirit do?
Nothing. The Book of Fate is closed to view.
Man, self-estranged, is enemy to man,
Knows not his origin, his place or plan,
Is a tormented atom, which at last
Must condescend to be the earth's repast;
Yes, but a thinking particle, whose eyes
Have measured the whole circuit of the skies.
We launch ourselves, like missiles, at the unknown,
Unknowing as we are, even of our own.
This theater-world of error, pride and stealth,
Is filled with invalids who discourse on health.
Seeking their good, men groan, complain and
    mourn,
Afraid of death, averse to being reborn.
Sometimes a glint of happiness appears
Among the shadows of this vale of tears,
But it takes wing, being itself a shade;
It is of loss and grief our lives are made.

The past is but a memory of despair,
The present ghastly if it points nowhere,
If the grave enfolds our spirit with our dust.
"Some day things will be well," there lies our
    trust.
"All's well today," is but the Seconal
Of the deluded; God alone knows all.
With humble sighs, resigned to pain, I raise
No shout or arrogant challenge to God's ways.
I struck a less lugubrious note when young;
Seductive pleasures rolled upon my tongue.
But styles change with the times; taught by old age,
Sharing the sickly human heritage,
In the soul's midnight, searching for one poor
    spark,
I've learned to suffer, silent, in the dark.
    A caliph once prayed in his last disease,
"I bring you, Lord, some curiosities
From our exotic regions here below:
Regrets and errors, ignorance and woe,
Unknown to the vast place where You exist."
He might have added *hope* to his grim list.

from the French of VOLTAIRE

FIFTH AVENUE PARADE

Vitrines of pearly gowns, bright porcelains,
Gilded dalmatics, the stone balconies
Of eminence, past all of these and past
The ghostly conquerors in swirls of bronze,
The children's pond, the Rospigliosi Cup,
Prinked with the glitter of day, the chrome batons
Of six high-stepping, slick drum-majorettes,
A local high school band in Robin's Egg Blue,
Envied by doormen, strippers, pianists,
Frogged with emblazonments, all smiles, advance
With victorious booms and fifings through a crowd
Flecked with balloons and flags and popsicles
Toward some weak, outnumbered, cowering North
That will lay down its arms at Eighty-sixth.

THE LULL

for *Allen Tate*

Through a loose camouflage
Of maples bowing gravely to everyone
In the neighborhood, and the soft, remote barrage
Of waterfalls or whispers, a stippled sun
Staggers about our garden, high
On the clear morning wines of mid-July.

Caught on a lifting tide
Above a spill of doubloons that drift together
Through the lawn's shoals and shadows, branches
ride
The sways of lime and gold, or dip and feather
The millrace waterways to soar
Over a tiled and tessellated floor.

A casual, leafy sprawl
Of floated lights, of waverings, these are
Swags of mimosan gentleness, and all
The quiet, bourgeois riches of Bonnard.
Or were, until just now the air
Came to a sudden hush, and everywhere

Things harden to an etched
And iron immobility, as day
Fades from a scurry of color to cross-hatched,
Sullen industrial tones of snapshot gray.
Instinctively the mind withdraws
To airports, depots, the long, plotless pause

Between the acts of a play,
Those neuter, intermediary states
Of vacancy and tedium and delay
When it must wait and wait, as now it waits
For a Wagnerian storm to roll
Thunder along the street and drench the soul.

Meanwhile, the trustful eye,
Content to notice merely what is there,
Remarks the ghostly phosphors of the sky,
The cast of mercury vapor everywhere—
Some shadowless, unfocussed light
In which all things come into their own right,

Pebble and weed and leaf
Distinct, refreshed, and cleanly self-defined,
Rapt in a trance of stillness, in a brief
Mood of serenity, as if designed
To be here now, and manifest
The deep, unvexed composure of the blessed.

The seamed, impastoed bark,
The cool, imperial certainty of stone,
Antique leaf-lace, all these are bathed in a dark
Mushroom and mineral odor of their own,
Their inwardness made clear and sure
As voice and fingerprint and signature.

The rain, of course, will come
With grandstand flourishes and hullabaloo,
The silvered streets, flashbulb and kettledrum,
To douse and rouse the citizens, to strew
Its rhinestones randomly, piecemeal.
But for the moment the whole world is real.

THE VENETIAN VESPERS

For HELEN

Whatever pain is figured in these pages
  Whatever voice here grieves,
Belonged to other lives and distant ages
  Mnemosyne retrieves;
But all the joys and forces of invention
  That can transmute to true
Gold these base matters floated in suspension
  Are due alone to you.

Thou must be patient. We came crying hither;
Thou know'st, the first time that we smell the air
We wawl and cry.

King Lear, IV, vi, 182–4

Though in many of its aspects this visible world seems
formed in love, the invisible spheres were formed in fright.

Moby Dick, CH. XLII

Muss es sein?
Es muss sein!
Es muss sein!
BEETHOVEN, *Quartet #16 in F major,*
opus 135

I

THE GRAPES

At five o'clock of a summer afternoon
We are already shadowed by the mountain
On whose lower slopes we perch, all of us here
At the *Hôtel de l'Univers et Déjeuner.*
The fruit trees and the stone lions out front
In deepening purple silhouette themselves
Against the bright green fields across the valley
Where, at the *Beau Rivage,* patrons are laved
In generous tides of gold. At cocktail time
Their glasses glint like gems, while we're eclipsed.
Which may explain
Why the younger set, which likes to get up late,
Assess its members over aperitifs,
Prefers that western slope, while we attract
A somewhat older, quieter clientele,
Americans mostly, though they seem to come
From everywhere, and are usually good tippers.
Still, it is strange and sad, at cocktail time,
To look across the valley from our shade,
As if from premature death, at all that brilliance
Across which silently on certain days
Shadows of clouds slide past in smooth parade,
While even our daisies and white irises
Are filled with blues and darkened premonitions.
Yet for our patrons, who are on holiday,
Questions of time are largely set aside.
They are indulgently amused to find
All the news magazines on the wicker table
In the lobby are outrageously outdated.
But Madame likes to keep them on display;
They add a touch of color, and a note
Of home and habit for many, and it's surprising
How thoroughly they are read on rainy days.
And I myself have smuggled one or two
Up to my bedroom, there to browse upon
Arrested time in *Time, Incorporated.*

There it is always 1954,
And Marlon Brando, perfectly preserved,
Sullen and brutal and desirable,
Avoids my eyes with a scowl; the record mile
Always belongs to Roger Bannister;
The rich and sleek of the international set
Are robbed of their furs and diamonds, get divorced
In a world so far removed from the rest of us
It almost seems arranged for our amusement
As they pose for pictures, perfectly made-up,
Coiffeured by Mr. Charles, languid, serene.
They never show up here—our little resort
Is far too mean for them—except in my daydreams.
My dreams at night are reserved for Marc-Antoine,
One of the bellboys at the *Beau Rivage.*
In his striped vest with flat buttons of brass
He comes to me every night after my prayers,
In fantasy, of course; in actual fact
He's taken no notice of me whatsoever.
Quite understandable, for I must be
Easily ten years older than he, and only
A chambermaid. As with all the very young,
To him the future's limitless and bright,
Anything's possible, one has but to wait.
No doubt it explains his native cheerfulness.
No doubt he dreams of a young millionairess,
Beautiful, spoiled and ardent, at his feet.
Perhaps it shall come to pass. Such things have happened.
Even barmaids and pantry girls have been seen
Translated into starlets tanning themselves
At the end of a diving board. But just this morning
Something came over me like the discovery
Of a deep secret of the universe.
It was early. I was in the dining room
Long before breakfast was served. I was alone.
Mornings, of course, it's we who get the light,
An especially tender light, hopeful and soft.

I stood beside a table near a window,
Gazing down at a crystal bowl of grapes
In ice-water. They were green grapes, or, rather,
They were a sort of pure, unblemished jade,
Like turbulent ocean water, with misted skins,
Their own pale, smoky sweat, or tiny frost.
I leaned over the table, letting the sun
Fall on my forearm, contemplating them.
Reflections of the water dodged and swam
In nervous incandescent filaments
Over my blouse and up along the ceiling.
And all those little bags of glassiness,
Those clustered planets, leaned their eastern cheeks
Into the sunlight, each one showing a soft
Meridian swelling where the thinning light
Mysteriously tapered into shadow,
To cool recesses, to the tranquil blues
That then were pillowing the *Beau Rivage*.
And watching I could almost see the light
Edge slowly over their simple surfaces,
And feel the sunlight moving on my skin
Like a warm glacier. And I seemed to know
In my blood the meaning of sidereal time
And know my little life had somehow crested.
There was nothing left for me now, nothing but years.
My destiny was cast and Marc-Antoine
Would not be called to play a part in it.
His passion, his Dark Queen, he'd meet elsewhere.
And I knew at last, with a faint, visceral twitch,
A flood of weakness that comes to the resigned,
What it must have felt like in that rubber boat
In mid-Pacific, to be the sole survivor
Of a crash, idly dandled on that blank
Untroubled waste, and see the light decline,
Taper and fade in graduated shades
Behind the International Date Line—
An accident I read about in *Time*.

THE DEODAND

What are these women up to? They've gone and strung
Drapes over the windows, cutting out light
And the slightest hope of a breeze here in mid-August.
Can this be simply to avoid being seen
By some prying *femme-de-chambre* across the boulevard
Who has stepped out on a balcony to disburse
Her dustmop gleanings on the summer air?
And what of these rugs and pillows, all haphazard,
Here in what might be someone's living room
In the swank, high-toned sixteenth *arrondissement?*
What would their fathers, husbands, *fiancés,*
Those pillars of the old *haute-bourgeoisie,*
Think of the strange charade now in the making?
Swathed in exotic finery, in loose silks,
Gauzy organzas with metallic threads,
Intricate Arab vests, brass ornaments
At wrist and ankle, those small sexual fetters,
Tight little silver chains, and bangled gold
Suspended like a coarse barbarian treasure
From soft earlobes pierced through symbolically,
They are preparing some *tableau vivant.*
One girl, consulting the authority
Of a painting, perhaps by Ingres or Delacroix,
Is reporting over her shoulder on the use
Of kohl to lend its dark, savage allurements.
Another, playing the slave-artisan's role,
Almost completely naked, brush in hand,
Attends to these instructions as she prepares
To complete the seductive shadowing of the eyes
Of the blonde girl who appears the harem favorite,
And who is now admiring these effects
In a mirror held by a fourth, a well-clad servant.
The scene simmers with Paris and women in heat,
Darkened and airless, perhaps with a faint hum
Of trapped flies, and a strong odor of musk.
For whom do they play at this hot indolence

And languorous vassalage? They are alone
With fantasies of jasmine and brass lamps,
Melons and dates and bowls of rose-water,
A courtyard fountain's firework blaze of prisms,
Its basin sown with stars and *poissons d'or*,
And a rude stable smell of animal strength,
Of leather thongs, hinting of violations,
Swooning lubricities and lassitudes.
What is all this but crude imperial pride,
Feminized, scented and attenuated,
The exploitation of the primitive,
Homages of romantic self-deception,
Mimes of submission glamorized as lust?
Have they no intimation, no recall
Of the once queen who liked to play at milkmaid,
And the fierce butcher-reckoning that followed
Her innocent, unthinking masquerade?
Those who will not be taught by history
Have as their curse the office to repeat it,
And for this little spiritual debauch
(Reported here with warm, exacting care
By Pierre Renoir in 1872—
Apparently unnoticed by the girls,
An invisible voyeur, like you and me)
Exactions shall be made, an expiation,
A forfeiture. Though it take ninety years,
All the retributive iron of Racine
Shall answer from the raging heat of the desert.

In the final months of the Algerian war
They captured a very young French Legionnaire.
They shaved his head, decked him in a blonde wig,
Carmined his lips grotesquely, fitted him out
With long, theatrical false eyelashes
And a bright, loose-fitting skirt of calico,
And cut off all the fingers of both hands.
He had to eat from a fork held by his captors.

Thus costumed, he was taken from town to town,
Encampment to encampment, on a leash,
And forced to beg for his food with a special verse
Sung to a popular show tune of those days :
"*Donnez moi à manger de vos mains*
Car c'est pour vous que je fais ma petite danse;
Car je suis Madeleine, la putain,
Et je m'en vais le lendemain matin,
Car je suis La Belle France."

THE SHORT END

Here the anthem doth commence:
Love and Constancy is dead,
Phoenix and the turtle fled
In a mutual flame from hence.

I

"Greetings from Tijuana!" on a ground
Of ripe banana rayon with a fat
And couchant Mexican in mid-siesta,
Wrapped in a many-colored Jacobin
Serape, and more deeply rapt in sleep,
Head propped against a phallic organ cactus
Of shamrock green, all thrown against a throw
Of purple on a Biedermeier couch—
This is the latest prize, newly unwrapped,
A bright and shiny capstone to the largest
Assemblage of such pillows in the East:
Pillows from Kennebunkport, balsam-scented
And stuffed with woodchips, pillows from Coney Island
Blazoned with Ferris Wheels and Roller Coasters,
Pillows that fart when sat on, tasselled pillows
From Old New Orleans, creole and redly carnal,
And what may be the gem of the collection,
From the New York World's Fair of Thirty-Nine,
Bearing a white Trylon and Perisphere,
Moderne, severe and thrilling, on the recto;
And on the verso in gold and blue italics
The Fair's motto: "A Century of Progress."
To this exciting find, picked up for pennies
At a garage sale in Schenectady
(Though slightly soiled with ketchup at one corner)
Yosemite, Niagara, Honolulu
Have yielded place, meekly accepting exile
In the mud room, the conversation pit,
Or other unpeopled but bepillowed rooms.

The Short End

This far-flung empire, these domains belong
To Shirley Carson and her husband, "Kit,"
Softening the hard edges of their lives.
Shirley is curator, museum guide,
The Mellon and the Berenson of these
Mute instances (except for the hidden farts)
Of fustian and of bombast, crocheted, embroidered
And stencilled with bright Day-Glo coloring.
They cheer her with their brilliance, with their sleek
And traveled worldliness, and serve as cover,
In the literal sense, a plumped and bolstered cover,
For the booze she needs to have always at hand.
There used to be a game, long since abandoned,
In which he'd try to find what she concealed.
"Cooler," she'd say, "yer gettin' really icy,"
She'd say, "so whyantcha fix yerself a drink?"
As he sought vainly behind Acapulco,
All flame and orange satin, or underneath
A petit point of moviedom's nobility :
A famous, genuine Hollywood Marquee,
Below which stood a spurious Romanov.
He quit because she always had reserves,
What she called "liquid assets," tucked away.
He had tried everything over the years.
There was no appealing to her vanity;
She was now puffily fat and pillowy.
Reason, of course, was futile, and he'd learned
That strong-arm methods strengthened her defiance.
These days he came home from the body shop
He owned and operated, its walls thumb-tacked
With centerfolded bodies from *Playboy*,
Yielding, expectant, invitational,
Came home oil-stained and late to find her drunk
And the house rank with the staleness of dead butts.
Staleness, that's what it was, he used to say
To himself, trying to figure what went wrong,
Emptying ashtrays of their ghostly wreckage,

Their powders and cremations of the past.
He always went to bed long before she did.
She would sit up till late, smoking and drinking,
Afloat upon a wild surfeit of colors,
The midway braveries, harlequin streamers,
Or skewbald, carney liveries of the macaw,
Through which, from time to time, memories arose.

II

Of these, two were persistent. In one of them
She was back in the first, untainted months of marriage,
Slight, shy, and dressed in soft ecru charmeuse,
Hopeful, adoring, and in return adored
By her husband, who was then a traveling salesman.
The company had scheduled a convention
In Atlantic City, and had generously
Invited the men to bring along their wives.
They were to stay in triumph at the Marlborough-
Blenheim, a luxury resort hotel
That ran both fresh and salt water in its tubs,
And boasted an international string ensemble
That assembled every afternoon at four
For *thé dansant*, when the very air was rich
With Jerome Kern, Romberg, and Rudolph Friml.
The room they were assigned gave on an air shaft
But even so they could smell the black Atlantic,
And being hidden away, she told herself,
Was just the thing for newlyweds, and made
Forays on the interminable vista
Of the boardwalk—it seemed to stretch away
In hazy diminution, like the prospects
Or boxwood avenues of a chateau—
The more exciting. Or so it seemed in prospect.
She recalled the opulent soft wind-chime music,

A mingling of silverware and ice-water
At their first breakfast in the dining room.
Also another sound. That of men's voices
Just slightly louder than was necessary
For the table-mates they seemed to be addressing.
It bore some message, all that baritone
Brio of masculine snort and self-assertion.
It belonged with cigars and bets and locker rooms.
It had nothing to do with damask and chandeliers.
It was a sign, she knew at once, of something.
They wore her husband's same convention badge,
So must be salesmen, here for a pep talk
And booster from top-level management,
Young, hopeful, energetic, just like him,
But, in some way she found unnerving, louder.
That was the earliest omen.
                                        The second was
The vast boardwalk itself, its herringbone
Of seasoned lumber lined on the inland side
By Frozen Custard booths, Salt Water Taffy
Kneaded and stretched by large industrial cams,
Pinball and shooting galleries with Kewpie Dolls,
Pink dachshunds, cross-eyed ostriches for prizes,
Fun Houses, Bumpum Cars and bowling alleys,
And shops that offered the discriminating
Hand-decorated shells, fantastic landscapes
Entirely composed of varnished star-fish,
And other shops displaying what was called
"Sophisticated Nightwear For My Lady,"
With black-lace panties bearing a crimson heart
At what might be Mons Veneris' timber-line,
Flesh-toned brassieres with large rose-window cutouts
Edged with elaborate guimpe, rococo portholes
Allowing the nipples to assert themselves,
And see-through nightgowns bordered with angora
Or frowsy feather boas of magenta.
Here she was free to take the healthful airs,

Inhale the unclippered trade-winds of New Jersey
And otherwise romp and disport herself
From nine until five-thirty, when her husband,
Her only Norman, would be returned to her.
Such was this place, a hapless rural seat
And sandy edge of the Truck Garden State,
The dubious North American Paradise.

III

It was just after dinner their second evening
That a fellow-conventioneer, met in the lobby,
Invited them to join a little party
For a libation in the Plantagenet Bar
And Tap Room; he performed the introductions
To Madge and Felix, Bubbles and Billy Jim,
Astrid, and lastly, to himself, Maurice,
Whose nickname, it appeared, was Two Potato,
And things were on a genial, first-name basis
Right from the start, so it was only after
The second round of drinks (which both the Carsons
Intended as their last, and a sufficient
Fling at impromptu sociability)
That it was inadvertently discovered
That the Carsons were little more than newlyweds
On what amounted to their honeymoon.
No one would hear of them leaving, or trying to pay
For anything. Another round of drinks
Was ordered. Two Potato proclaimed himself
Their host, and winked at them emphatically.
There followed much raucous, suggestive toasting,
Norman was designated "a stripling kid,"
And ceremoniously nicknamed "Kit,"
And people started calling Shirley "Shirl,"
And "Curly-Shirl" and "Shirl-Girl." There were displays

Of mock-tenderness towards the young couple
And gags about the missionary position,
With weak, off-key, off-color, attempts at singing
"Rock of Ages," with hands clasped in prayer
And eyes raised ceilingward at "cleft for me,"
Eyes closed at "let me hide myself in thee,"
The whole number grotesquely harmonized
In the manner of a barbershop quartet.
By now she wanted desperately to leave
But couldn't figure out the way to do so
Without giving offense, seeming ungrateful;
And somehow, she suspected, they knew this.
Two Potato particularly seemed
Aggressive both in his solicitude
And in the smirking lewdness of his jokes
As he unblushingly eyed the bride for blushes
And gallantly declared her "a good sport,"
"A regular fella," and "the little woman."
She knew when the next round of drinks appeared
That she and Norman were mere hostages
Whom nobody would ransom. Billy Jim asked
If either of them knew a folk-song called
"The Old Gism Trail," and everybody laughed,
Laughed at the plain vulgarity itself
And at the Carsons' manifest discomfort
And at their pained, inept attempt at laughter.
The merriment was acid and complex.
Felix it was who kept proposing toasts
To "good ol' Shirl an' Kit," names which he slurred
Both in pronunciation and disparagement
With an expansive, wanton drunkenness
That in its license seemed soberly planned
To increase by graduated steps until
Without seeming aware of what he was doing
He'd raise a toast to "good ol' Curl an' Shit."
They managed to get away before that happened,
Though Shirley knew in her bones it was intended,

Had seen it coming from a mile away.
They left, but not before it was made clear
That they were the only married couple present,
That the other men had left their wives at home,
And that this was what conventions were all about.
The Carsons were made to feel laughably foolish,
Timid and prepubescent and repressed,
And with a final flourish of raised glasses
The "guests" were at last permitted to withdraw.

IV

    Fade-out; assisted by a dram of gin,
And a soft radio soundtrack bringing up
A velvety chanteur who wants a kiss
By wire, in some access of chastity,
Yet in a throaty passion volunteers,
"Baby, mah heart's on fire." Fade-in with pan
Shot of a highway somewhere south of Wheeling
Where she and her husband, whom she now calls Kit,
Were driving through a late day in November
Toward some goal obscure as the very weather,
Defunctive, moist, overcast, requiescent.
Rounding a bend, they came in sudden view
Of what seemed a caravan of trucks and cars,
A long civilian convoy, parked along
The right-hand shoulder, and instantly slowed down,
Fearing a speed-trap or an accident.
It was instead, as a billboard announced,
A LIVE ENTOMBMENT—CONTRIBUTIONS PLEASE.
They found a parking slot, directed by
Two courteous State Troopers with leather holsters
That seemed tumescent with heavy, flopping side-arms,
And made their way across the stony ground
To a strange, silent crowd, as at a grave-side.

A poster fixed to a tree gave the details :
"Here lies George Rose in a casket supplied by
The Memento Morey Funeral Home of Wheeling.
He has been underground 38 days.
[The place for the numbers was plastered with new stickers.]
He lives on liquids and almond Hershey bars
Fed through the speaking tube next to his head,
By which his brother and custodian,
John Wesley Rose, communicates with him,
And by means of which he breathes. Note that the tube
Can be bent sideways to keep out the rain.
Visitors are invited to put all questions
To the custodian because George Rose
Is eager to preserve his solitude.
He has forsworn the vanities of this world.
Donations will be gratefully accepted."
At length she wedged her way among the curious
To where she saw a varnished pine-wood box
With neatly mitred corners, fitted with glass
At the top, and measuring roughly a foot square,
Sunk in the earth, protruding about three inches.
Through this plain aperture she now beheld
The pale, expressionless features of George Rose,
Bearded, but with a pocked, pitted complexion,
And pale blue eyes conveying by their blankness
A boredom so profound it might indeed
Pass for a certain otherworldliness,
Making it eminently clear to all
That not a single face that showed itself
Against the sky for his consideration
Was found by him to be beautiful or wise
Or worthy of the least notice or interest.
One could tell he was alive because he blinked.
At the crowd's edge, near the collection box,
Stood a man who was almost certainly his brother,
Caretaker and custodian, engaged
In earnest talk with one of the State Troopers.

It crossed her mind to wonder how they dealt
With his evacuations, yet she couldn't
Ask such a question of an unknown man.
But Kit seemed to have questions of his own
And as he approached John Wesley she turned away
To the edge of a large field and stood alone
In some strange wordless seizure of distress.
She turned her gaze deliberately away
From the road, the cars, the little clustered knot
Of humankind around that sheet of glass,
Like flies around a dish of sweetened water,
And focused intently on what lay before her.
A grizzled landscape, burdock and thistle-choked,
A snarled, barbed-wire barricade of brambles,
All thorn and needle-sharp hostility.
The dead weeds wicker-brittle, raffia-pale,
The curled oak leaves a deep tobacco brown,
The sad rouge of old bricks, chips of cement
From broken masonry, a stubble field
Like a mangy lion's pelt of withered grass.
Off in the distance a thoroughly dead tree,
Peeled of its bark, sapless, an armature
Of well-groomed, military, silver-gray.
And other leafless trees, their smallest twigs
Incising a sky the color of a bruise.
In all the rancid, tannic, mustard tones,
Mud colors, lignum grays and mottled rocks,
The only visible relief she found
Was the plush red velvet of the sumac spikes
And the slick, vinyl, Stygian, anthracite
Blackness of water in a drainage ditch.
The air sang with the cold of empty caves,
Of mildew, cobwebs, slug and maggot life.
And at her feet, among the scattered stubs
Of water-logged non-filter cigarettes,
Lay a limp length of trampled fennel stalk.
And then she heard, astonishingly close,

Right at her side, the incontestable voice
Of someone who could not possibly be there :
Of old Miss McIntosh, her eleventh grade
Latin instructor, now many years dead,
Saying with slow, measured authority,
"It is your duty to remain right here.
Those people and their cars will go away.
Norman will go. George Rose will stay where he is,
But you have nothing whatever to do with him.
He will die quietly inside his coffin.
From time to time you will be given water
And a peanut butter sandwich on white bread.
You will stay here as long as it shall take
To love this place so much you elect to stay
Forever, forsaking all others you have known
Or dreamed of or incontinently longed for.
Look at and meditate upon the crows.
Think upon God. Humbly prepare yourself,
Like the wise virgins in the parable,
For the coming resurrection of George Rose.
Consider deeply why as the first example
Of the first conjugation—which is not
As conjugal as some suppose—one learns
The model verb forms of 'to love,' *amare,*
Which also happens to be the word for 'bitter.'
Both love and Latin are more difficult
Than is usually imagined or admitted.
This is your final exam; this is your classroom."

V

Another voice drowns out Miss McIntosh.
It's Mel Tormé, singing *Who's Sorry Now?*
Followed by a Kid Ory version of

Quincy Street Stomp, and bringing back in view
The bright upholstery of the present tense,
The lax geography of pillows, gin-
And-bitters with anesthetic bitterness.
It must be three AM, but never mind.
Open upon her lap lies *The New Yorker,*
Exhibiting a full-page color ad
For the Scotch whiskey-based liqueur, Drambuie,
Soft-focus, in the palest tints of dawn.
Therein a lady and a gentleman
Stand gazing north from the triumphal arch
That Stanford White designed for Washington Square.
She wears an evening gown of shocking pink
And a mink stole. Her escort, in black tie,
Standing behind her, his arms about her waist,
Follows her gaze uptown where a peach haze
Is about to infuse the windows of the rich.
Meanwhile, this couple, who have just descended
From a hansom cab departing towards the east,
Have all Fifth Avenue stretched out before them
In Élysée prospectus, like the calm fields
Where Attic heroes dwell. They are alone
On the blank street. The truths of economics,
The dismal (decimal) science, dissolve away
In the faint light, and leave her standing there,
Shirley herself, suddenly slim again,
In the arms of a young nameless gentleman.
To be sure, the salmon hues up in the eighties,
Flushing the Metropolitan's facade,
Glinting on silver tops of skyscrapers
As upon factory-made, hand-polished Alps
(Though the deep canyons still repose in darkness)
Bespeak the calm beneficence of dawn
When they shall both raise up their brandy glasses
Filled with that admirable Scotch liqueur
Or else with gin and tolerable bitters

And toast each other in some nearby penthouse.
But meanwhile her attention is wholly drawn
To the carriage lantern on the hansom cab.
A kerosene lantern with a concave shield
Or chrome reflector inside a box of glass.
The quivering flame of the broad ribbon wick
Itself presents a quick array of colors,
All brilliance, light, intensity and hope.
The flames flow upward from a rounded base
Like an inverted waterfall of gold,
Yet somehow at the center, the pure kernel
Of fire is pearly, incandescent white.
Out of that whiteness all the celestial hues
Of dawn proliferate in wobbly spectra,
Lilac and orange, the rust of marigold,
The warm and tropic colors of the world
That she inhabits, that she has collected
And stuffed like assorted trophies of the kill.
The shape of flames is almond-like, the shape
Of Egyptian eyes turned sideways, garlic cloves,
Camel-hair tips of watercolor brushes,
Of waterdrops. The shape performs a dance,
A sinuous, erotic wavering,
All inference and instability,
Shimmy and glitter. It is, she suddenly knows,
The figure *redivivus* of George Rose,
Arisen, youthful, strong and roseate,
Tiny, of course, pathetically reduced
To pinky size, but performing a lewd dance
Of Shiva, the rippling muscles of his thighs
And abdomen as fluent as a river
Of upward-pouring color, the golden finish
Of Sardanapalus, emphatic rhythms
Of blues and body language, a centrifuge
Of climbing braids that beautifully enlarge,
Thicken and hang pendulous in the air.
Out of these twinings, foldings, envelopings

Of brass and apricot, biceps and groin,
She sees the last thing she will ever see :
The purest red there is, passional red,
Fire-engine red, the red of Valentines,
Of which she is herself the howling center.

INVECTIVE AGAINST DENISE, A WITCH

The hatred I reserve for thee
Surpasses the malignity
    Of camel and of bear,
Old witch, unseemly thaumaturge,
Whipped by the Public Hangman's scourge
    The length of the town square.

Luring about you, like a brood,
The vulgar, curious and lewd,
    You shamelessly lay bare
Your haunches to the sight of men,
Your naked shoulder, abdomen
    Emblazoned with blood-smear.

And yet that punishment is slight
Compared to what is yours by right;
    Just Heaven must not bestow
Its mercy on so foul a thing
But rather by its whirlwind bring
    Such proud excesses low.

Still wracked by the brute overthrow
The Titans suffered long ago,
    A brooding Mother Earth,
To spite the Gods, in her old age
Shall, in an ecstasy of rage,
    At last bring you to birth.

You know the worth and power of both
Rare herbals and concocted broth
    Brought from the tropic zone;
You know the very month and hour
To pluck the lust-inducing flower
    That makes a woman groan.

There's not, among the envenomed plants
On mountain or in valley haunts,
      One that your eyes have missed
And has not yielded up its ground
To your bright sickle-blade, and crowned
      Your formidable quest.

When, like a lunatic, all bare,
The moon lets down its mystic hair
      Of cold, enraging light,
You wrap your features in the hide
Of animals, and smoothly glide
      Abroad into the night.

Your least breath ravishes the blood
Of all dogs in the neighborhood
      And sets them on to bark,
Makes rivers flow uphill, reversed,
And baying wolves observe your cursed
      Hegira through the dark.

Chatelaine of deserted spots,
Of mouldered cemetery plots
      Where you are most at home,
Muttering diabolic runes,
You disinter the troubled bones
      From their sequestered tomb.

To grieve a mother more you don
The aspect of her only son
      Who has just met his death,
And you assume the very shape
That makes an aged widow gape
      And robs her of her breath.

You make the spell-bound moon appear
To march through the all-silvered air,
    And cast through midnight's hush
Such tincture on a pallid face
A thousand-cymbaled crashing brass
    Could not restore its flush.

The terror of us all, we fear
Your hateful practice, and we bar
    Your presence from our door,
Afraid you will inflict a pox
Upon our persons, herds and flocks,
    With juice of hellebore.

Often I've watched as you espy
From far away with baleful eye
    Some shepherd on his heights;
Soon after, victim of your arts,
The man is dead, his fleshly parts
    A nest of parasites.

And yet like vile Medea, you
Could sometimes prove life-giving, too;
    You know what secret thing
Gave Aeson back his sapling youth,
Yet by your spells you have in truth
    Deprived me of my spring.

O Gods, if pity dwells on high,
May her requital be to die,
    And may her last repose,
Unblessed by burial, serve as feast
To every gross and shameful beast,
    To jackals and to crows.

(FROM PIERRE DE RONSARD)

AUSPICES

Cold, blustery cider weather, the flat fields
Bleached pale as straw, the leaves, such as remain,
Pumpkin or leather-brown. These are the wilds
Of loneliness, huge, vacant, sour and plain.

The sky is hourless dusk, portending rain.
Or perhaps snow. This narrow footpath edges
A small stand of scrub pine, warped as with pain,
And baneberry lofts its little poisoned pledges.

The footpath ends in a dried waterhole,
Plastered with black like old tar-paper siding.
The fearfullest desolations of the soul
Image themselves as local and abiding.

Even if I should get away from here
My trouser legs are stuck with burrs and seeds,
Grappled and spiked reminders of my fear,
Standing alone among the beggarweeds.

APPLICATION FOR A GRANT

Noble executors of the munificent testament
Of the late John Simon Guggenheim, distinguished bunch
Of benefactors, there are certain kinds of men
Who set their hearts on being bartenders,
For whom a life upon duck-boards, among fifths,
Tapped kegs and lemon twists, crowded with lushes
Who can master neither their bladders nor consonants,
Is the only life, greatly to be desired.
There's the man who yearns for the White House, there to
    compose
Rhythmical lists of enemies, while someone else
Wants to be known to the *Tour d'Argent's* head waiter.
As the Sibyl of Cumae said : It takes all kinds.
Nothing could bribe your Timon, your charter member
Of the Fraternal Order of Grizzly Bears to love
His fellow, whereas it's just the opposite
With interior decorators; that's what makes horse races.
One man may have a sharp nose for tax shelters,
Screwing the IRS with mirth and profit;
Another devote himself to his shell collection,
Deaf to his offspring, indifferent to the feast
With which his wife hopes to attract his notice.
Some at the Health Club sweating under bar bells
Labor away like grunting troglodytes,
Smelly and thick and inarticulate,
Their brains squeezed out through their pores by sheer
    exertion.
As for me, the prize for poets, the simple gift
For amphybrachs strewn by a kind Euterpe,
With perhaps a laurel crown of the evergreen
Imperishable of your fine endowment
Would supply my modest wants, who dream of nothing
But a pad on Eighth Street and your approbation.

(FREELY FROM HORACE)

AN OVERVIEW

Here, god-like, in a 707,
As on an air-conditioned cloud,
One knows the frailties of the proud
And comprehends the Fall from Heaven.

The world, its highways, trees and ports,
Looks much as if it were designed
With nifty model trains in mind
By salesmen at F. A. O. Schwarz.

Such the enchantment distance lends.
The bridges, matchstick and minute,
Seem faultless, intricate and cute,
Contrived for slight, aesthetic ends.

No wonder the camaraderie
Of mission-happy Air Force boys
Above so vast a spread of toys,
Cruising the skies, lighthearted, free,

Or the engaging roguishness
With which a youthful bombardier
Unloads his eggs on what appear
The perfect patchwork squares of chess;

Nor that the brass hat general staff,
Tailored and polished to a fault,
Favor an undeclared assault
On what an aerial photograph

Shows as an unstrung ball of twine,
Or that the President insist
A nation colored amethyst
Should bow to his supreme design.

But in the toy store, right up close,
Chipped paint and mucilage represent
The wounded, orphaned, indigent,
The dying and the comatose.

STILL LIFE

Sleep-walking vapor, like a visitant ghost,
      Hovers above a lake
Of Tennysonian calm just before dawn.
Inverted trees and boulders waver and coast
In polished darkness. Glints of silver break
Among the liquid leafage, and then are gone.

Everything's doused and diamonded with wet.
      A cobweb, woven taut
On bending stanchion frames of tentpole grass,
Sags like a trampoline or firemen's net
With all the glitter and riches it has caught,
Each drop a paperweight of Steuben glass.

No birdsong yet, no cricket, nor does the trout
      Explode in water-scrolls
For a skimming fly. All that is yet to come.
Things are as still and motionless throughout
The universe as ancient Chinese bowls,
And nature is magnificently dumb.

Why does this so much stir me, like a code
      Or muffled intimation
Of purposes and preordained events?
It knows me, and I recognize its mode
Of cautionary, spring-tight hesitation,
This silence so impacted and intense.

As in a water-surface I behold
      The first, soft, peach decree
Of light, its pale, inaudible commands.
I stand beneath a pine-tree in the cold,
Just before dawn, somewhere in Germany,
A cold, wet, Garand rifle in my hands.

PERSISTENCES

The leafless trees are feathery,
    A foxed, Victorian lace,
Against a sky of milk-glass blue,
    Blank, washed-out, commonplace.

Between them and my window
    Huge helices of snow
Perform their savage, churning rites
    At seventeen below.

The obscurity resembles
    A silken Chinese mist
Wherein through calligraphic daubs
    Of artistry persist

Pocked and volcanic gorges,
    Clenched and arthritic pines,
Faint, coral-tinted herons' legs
    Splashing among the tines

Of waving, tasselled marshgrass,
    Deep pools aflash with sharp,
Shingled and burnished armor-plate
    Of sacred, child-eyed carp.

This dimness is dynastic,
    An ashen T'ang of age
Or blur that grudgingly reveals
    A ghostly equipage,

Ancestral deputations
    Wound in the whited air,
To whom some sentry flings a slight,
    Prescriptive, "Who goes there?"

Are these the apparitions
   Of enemies or friends?
Loved ones from whom I once withheld
   Kindnesses or amends

On preterite occasions
   Now lost beyond repeal?
Or the old childhood torturers
   Of undiminished zeal,

Adults who ridiculed me,
   Schoolmates who broke my nose,
Risen from black, unconscious depths
   Of REM repose?

Who comes here seeking justice,
   Or in its high despite,
Bent on some hopeless interview
   On wrongs nothing can right?

Those throngs disdain to answer,
   Though numberless as flakes;
Mine is the task to find out words
   For their memorial sakes

Who press in dense approaches,
   Blue numeral tattoos
Writ crosswise on their arteries,
   The burning, voiceless Jews.

A CAST OF LIGHT

at a Father's Day picnic

A maple bough of web-foot, golden greens,
      Found by an angled shaft
Of late sunlight, disposed within that shed
Radiance, with brilliant, hoisted baldachins,
Pup tents and canopies by some underdraft
Flung up to scattered perches overhead,

These daubs of sourball lime, at floating rest,
      Present to the loose wattage
Of heaven their limelit flukes, an artifice
Of archipelagian Islands of the Blessed,
And in all innocence pursue their cottage
Industry of photosynthesis.

Yet only for twenty minutes or so today,
      On a summer afternoon,
Does the splendid lancet reach to them, or sink
To these dim bottoms, making its chancy way,
As through the barrier reef of some lagoon
In sea-green darkness, by a wavering chink,

Down, neatly probing like an accurate paw
      Or a notched and beveled key,
Through the huge cave-roof of giant oak and pine.
And the heart goes numb in a tide of fear and awe
For those we cherish, their hopes, their frailty,
Their shadowy fate's unfathomable design.

HOUSE SPARROWS

for Joe and U. T. Summers

Not of the wealthy, Coral Gables class
Of travelers, nor that rarified tax bracket,
These birds weathered the brutal, wind-chill facts
Under our eaves, nesting in withered grass,
Wormless but hopeful, and now their voice enacts
Forsythian spring with primavernal racket.

Their color is the elderly, moleskin gray
Of doggedness, of mist, magnolia bark.
Salt of the earth, they are; the common clay;
Meek *émigrés* come over on the Ark
In steerage from the Old Country of the Drowned
To settle down along Long Island Sound,

Flatbush, Weehawken, our brownstone tenements,
Wherever the local idiom is *Cheep.*
Savers of string, meticulous and mild,
They are given to nervous flight, the troubled sleep
Of those who remember terrible events,
The wide-eyed, anxious haste of the exiled.

Like all the poor, their safety lies in numbers
And hardihood and anonymity
In a world of dripping browns and duns and umbers.
They have inherited the lower sky,
Their Lake of Constants, their blue modality
That they are borne upon and battered by.

Those little shin-bones, hollow at the core,
Emaciate finger-joints, those fleshless wrists,
Wrapped in a wrinkled, loose, rice-paper skin,
As though the harvests of earth had never been,
Where have we seen such frailty before?
In pictures of Biafra and Auschwitz.

Yet here they are, these chipper stratoliners,
Unsullen, unresentful, full of the grace
Of cheerfulness, who seem to greet all comers
With the wild confidence of Forty-Niners,
And, to the lively honor of their race,
Rude canticles of "Summers, Summers, Summers."

AN OLD MALEDICTION

What well-heeled knuckle-head, straight from the unisex
Hairstylist and bathed in *Russian Leather*,
Dallies with you these late summer days, Pyrrha,
In your expensive sublet? For whom do you
Slip into something simple by, say, Gucci?
The more fool he who has mapped out for himself
The saline latitudes of incontinent grief.
Dazzled though he be, poor dope, by the golden looks
Your locks fetched up out of a bottle of *Clairol*,
He will know that the wind changes, the smooth sailing
Is done for, when the breakers wallop him broadside,
When he's rudderless, dismasted, thoroughly swamped
In that mindless rip-tide that got the best of me
Once, when I ventured on your deeps, Piranha.

(FREELY FROM HORACE)

II

THE VENETIAN VESPERS

for Harry and Kathleen Ford

. . where's that palace whereinto foul things
Sometimes intrude not? Who has a breast so pure
But some uncleanly apprehensions
Keep leets and law days, and in session sit
With meditations lawful?
Othello: III, iii, 136–41

We cannot all have our gardens now, nor our
pleasant fields to meditate in at eventide.
RUSKIN: *The Stones of Venice,*
BK. I, CH. XXX

I

What's merciful is not knowing where you are,
What time it is, even your name or age,
But merely a clean coolness at the temple—
That, says the spirit softly, is enough
For the mind to adventure on its half-hidden path
Like starlight interrupted by dense trees
Journeying backwards on a winter trip
While you are going, as you fancy, forward,
And the stars are keeping pace with everything.
Where to begin? With the white, wrinkled membrane,
The disgusting skin that gathers on hot milk?
Or narrow slabs of jasper light at sundown
That fit themselves softly around the legs
Of chairs, and entertain a drift of motes,
A tide of sadness, a failing, a dying fall?
Or the glass jar, like a wet cell battery,
Full of electric coils and boiling resins,
Its tin Pinocchio nose with one small nostril,
And both of us under a tent of towels

Like child conspirators, the tin nose breathing
Health at me steadily, like the insufflation of God?
Yes, but also the sight, on a gray morning,
Beneath the crossbar of an iron railing
Painted a glossy black, of six waterdrops
Slung in suspension, sucking into themselves,
As if it were some morbid nourishment,
The sagging blackness of the rail itself,
But edged with brilliant fingernails of chrome
In which the world was wonderfully disfigured
Like faces seen in spoons, like mirrorings
In the fine spawn, the roe of air bubbles,
That tiny silver wampum along the stems,
Yellowed and magnified, of aging flowers
Caught in the lens of stale water and glass
In the upstairs room when somebody had died.
Just like the beads they sprinkled over cookies
At Christmas. Or perhaps those secret faces
Known to no one but me, slyly revealed
In repetitions of the wallpaper,
My tight network of agents in the field.
Well, yes. Any of these might somehow serve
As a departure point. But, perhaps, best
Would be those first precocious hints of hell,
Those intuitions of living desolation
That last a lifetime. These were never, for me,
Some desert place that humans had avoided
In which I could get lost, to which I might
In dreams condemn myself—a wilderness
Natural but alien and unpitying.
They were instead those derelict waste places
Abandoned by mankind as of no worth,
Frequented, if at all, by the dispossessed,
Nocturnal shapes, the crippled and the shamed.
Here in the haywire weeds, concealed by wilds
Of goldenrod and toadflax, lies a spur
With its one boxcar of brick-colored armor,

At noon, midsummer, fiercer than a kiln,
Rippling the thinness of the air around it
With visible distortions. Among the stones
Of the railbed, fragments of shattered amber
That held a pint of rye. The carapace
Of a dried beetle. A broken orange crate
Streaked with tobacco stains at the nailheads
In the gray, fractured slats. And over all
The dust of oblivion finer than milled flour
Where chips of brick, clinkers and old iron
Burn in their slow, invisible decay.
Or else it is late afternoon in autumn,
The sunlight rusting on the western fronts
Of a long block of Victorian brick houses,
Untenanted, presumably condemned,
Their brownstone grapes, their grand entablatures,
Their straining caryatid muscle-men
Rendered at once ridiculous and sad
By the black scars of zigzag fire escapes
That double themselves in isometric shadows.
And all their vacancy is given voice
By the endless flapping of one window-shade.
And then there is the rank, familiar smell
Of underpasses, the dark piers of bridges,
Where old men, the incontinent, urinate.
The acid smell of poverty, the jest
Of adolescent boys exchanging quips
About bedpans, the motorman's comfort,
A hospital world of syphons and thick tubes
That they know nothing of. Nor do they know
The heatless burnings of the elderly
In memorized, imaginary lusts,
Visions of noontide infidelities,
Crude hallway gropings, cruel lubricities,
A fire as cold and slow as rusting metal.
It's but a child's step, it's but an old man's totter
From this to the appalling world of dreams.

Gray bottled babies in formaldehyde
As in their primal amniotic bath.
Pale dowagers hiding their liver-spots
In a fine chalk, confectionery dust.
And then the unbearable close-up of a wart
With a tough bristle of hair, like a small beast
With head and feet tucked under, playing possum.
A meat-hooked ham, hung like a traitor's head
For the public's notice in a butcher shop,
Faintly resembling the gartered thigh
Of an acrobatic, overweight soubrette.
And a scaled, crusted animal whose head
Fits in a Nazi helmet, whose webbed feet
Are cold on the white flanks of dreaming lovers,
While thorned and furry legs embrace each other
As black mandibles tick. Immature girls,
Naked but for the stockings they stretch tight
To tempt the mucid glitter of an eye.
And the truncated snout of a small bat,
Like one whose nose, undermined by the pox,
Falls back to the skull's socket. Deepest of all,
Like the converging lines in diagrams
Of vanishing points, those underwater blades,
Those quills or sunburst spokes of marine light,
Flutings and gilded shafts in which one sees
In the drowned star of intersecting beams
Just at that final moment of suffocation
The terrifying and unmeaning rictus
Of the sandshark's stretched, involuntary grin.
In the upstairs room, when somebody had died,
There were flowers, there were underwater globes,
Mercury seedpearls. It was my mother died.
After a long illness and long ago.

San Pantaleone, heavenly buffoon,
Patron of dotards and of gondolas,
Forgive us the obsessional daydream

Of our redemption at work in black and white,
The silent movie, the old *Commedia*,
Which for the sake of the children in the house
The projectionist has ventured to run backwards.
(The reels must be rewound in any case.)
It is because of jumped, elided frames
That people make their way by jigs and spasms,
Impetuous leapings, violent semaphores,
Side-slipping, drunk discontinuities,
Like the staggered, tossed career of butterflies.
Here, in pure satisfaction of our hunger,
The Keystone Cops sprint from hysteria,
From brisk, slaphappy bludgeonings of crime,
Faultlessly backwards into calm patrol;
And gallons of spilled paint, meekly obedient
As a domestic pet, home in and settle
Securely into casually offered pails,
Leaving the Persian rugs immaculate.
But best of all are the magically dry legs
Emerging from a sudden crater of water
That closes itself up like a healed wound
To plate-glass polish as the diver slides
Upwards, attaining with careless arrogance
His unsought footing on the highest board.
Something profoundly soiled, pointlessly hurt
And beyond cure in us yearns for this costless
Ablution, this impossible reprieve,
Unpurchased at a scaffold, free, bequeathed
As rain upon the just and the unjust,
As in the fall of mercy, unconstrained,
Upon the poor, infected place beneath.

II

      Elsewhere the spirit is summoned back to life
By bells sifted through floating schools and splices
Of sun-splashed poplar leaves, a reverie
Of light chromatics (Monet and Debussy),
Or the intemperate storms and squalls of traffic,
The coarse, unanswered voice of a fog horn,
Or, best, the shy, experimental aubade
Of the first birds to sense that ashen cold
Grisaille from which the phoenix dawn arises.
Summoned, that is to say, to the world's life
From Piranesian *Carceri* and rat holes
Of its own deep contriving. But here in Venice,
The world's most louche and artificial city,
(In which my tale some time will peter out)
The summons comes from the harsh smashing of glass.
A not unsuitable local industry,
Being the frugal and space-saving work
Of the young men who run the garbage scows.
Wine bottles of a clear sea-water green,
Pale, smoky quarts of *acqua minerale*,
Iodine-tinted liters, the true-blue
Waterman's midnight ink of Bromo Seltzer,
Light-bulbs of packaged fog, fluorescent tubes
Of well-sealed, antiseptic samples of cloud,
Await what is at once their liquidation
And resurrection in the glory holes
Of the Murano furnaces. Meanwhile
Space must be made for all ephemera,
Our cast-offs, foulings, whatever has gone soft
With age, or age has hardened to a stone,
Our city sweepings. Venice has no curbs
At which to curb a dog, so underfoot
The ochre pastes and puddings of dogshit
Keep us earthbound in half a dozen ways,
Curbing the spirit's tendency to pride.

The palaces decay. Venice is rich
Chiefly in the deposits of her dogs.
A wealth swept up and gathered with its makers.
Canaries, mutts, love-birds and alley cats
Are sacked away like so many Monte Cristos,
There being neither lawns, meadows nor hillsides
To fertilize or to be buried in.
For them the glass is broken in the dark
As a remembrance by the garbage men.
I am their mourner at collection time
With an invented litany of my own.
Wagner died here, Stravinsky's buried here,
They say that Cimarosa's enemies
Poisoned him here. The mind at four AM
Is a poor, blotched, vermiculated thing.
I've seen it spilled like sweetbreads, and I've dreamed
Of Byron writing, "Many a fine day
I should have blown my brains out but for the thought
Of the pleasure it would give my mother-in-law."
Thus virtues, it is said, are forced upon us
By our own impudent crimes. I think of him
With his consorts of whores and countesses
Smelling of animal musk, lilac and garlic,
A *ménage* that was in fact a menagerie,
A fox, a wolf, a mastiff, birds and monkeys,
Corbaccios and corvinos, *spintriae*,
The lees of the Venetian underworld,
A plague of iridescent flies. Spilled out.
O lights and livers. Deader than dead weight.
In a casket lined with tufted tea-rose silk.
O that the soul should tie its shoes, the mind
Should wash its hands in a sink, that a small grain
Of immortality should fit itself
With dentures. We slip down by grades and degrees,
Lapses of memory, the vacant eye
And spittled lip, by soiled humiliations
Of mind and body into the last ditch,

Passing, en route to the *Incurabili*,
The backwater way stations of the soul,
Conveyed in the glossy hearse-and-coffin black
And soundless gondola by an overpriced
Apprentice Charon to the *Calle dei Morti*.
One approaches the Venetian underworld
Silently and by water, the gondolier
Creating eddies and whirlpools with each stroke
Like oak roots, silver, smooth and muscular.
One slides to it like a swoon, nearing the regions
Where the vast hosts of the dead mutely inhabit,
Pulseless, indifferent, deeply beyond caring
What shape intrudes itself upon their fathoms.
The oar-blade flings broadcast its beads of light,
Its ordinary gems. One travels past
All of these domiciles of raw sienna,
Burnt umber, colors of the whole world's clays.
One's weakness in itself becomes delicious
Towards the end, a kindly vacancy.
(Raise both your arms above your head, and then
Take three deep breaths, holding the third. Your partner,
Your childhood guide into the other world,
Will approach from behind and wrap you in a bear hug,
Squeezing with all his might. Your head will seethe
With prickled numbness, like an arm or leg
From which the circulation is cut off,
The lungs turn warm with pain, and then you slip
Into a velvet darkness, mutely grateful
To your Anubis-executioner . . .)
Probably I shall die here unremarked
Amid the albergo's seedy furniture,
Aware to the last of the faintly rotten scent
Of swamp and sea, a brief embarrassment
And nuisance to the management and the maid.
That would be bad enough without the fear
Byron confessed to : "If I should reach old age
I'll die 'at the top first,' like Swift." Or Swift's

Lightning-struck tree. There was a visitor,
The little Swiss authority on nightmares,
Young Henry Fuseli, who at thirty-one
Suffered a fever here for several days
From which he recovered with his hair turned white
As a judicial wig, and rendered permanently
Left-handed. And His Majesty, George III,
Desired the better acquaintance of a tree
At Windsor, and heartily shook one of its branches,
Taking it for the King of Prussia. Laugh
Whoso will that has no knowledge of
The violent ward. They subdued that one
With a hypodermic, quickly tranquilized
And trussed him like a fowl. These days I find
A small aperitif at Florian's
Is helpful, although I do not forget.
My views are much like Fuseli's, who described
His method thus : "I first sits myself down.
I then works myself up. Then I throws in
My darks. And then I takes away my lights."
His nightmare was a great success, while mine
Plays on the ceiling of my rented room
Or on the bone concavity of my skull
In the dark hours when I take away my lights.

      Lights. I have chosen Venice for its light,
Its lightness, buoyancy, its calm suspension
In time and water, its strange quietness.
I, an expatriate American,
Living off an annuity, confront
The lagoon's waters in mid-morning sun.
Palladio's church floats at its anchored peace
Across from me, and the great church of Health,
Voted in gratitude by the Venetians
For heavenly deliverance from the plague,
Voluted, levels itself on the canal.
Further away the bevels coil and join

Like spiraled cordon ropes of silk, the lips
Of the crimped water sped by a light breeze.
Morning has tooled the bay with bright inlays
Of writhing silver, scattered scintillance.
These little crests and ripples promenade,
Hurried and jocular and never bored,
Ils se promènent like families of some means
On Sundays in the *Bois.* Observing this
Easy festivity, hypnotized by
Tiny sun-signals exchanged across the harbor,
I am for the moment cured of everything,
The future held at bay, the past submerged,
Even the fact that this Sea of Hadria,
This consecrated, cool wife of the Doge,
Was ploughed by the merchantmen of all the world,
And all the silicate fragility
They sweat for at the furnaces now seems
An admirable and shatterable triumph.
They take the first crude bulb of thickened glass,
Glowing and taffy-soft on the blow tube,
And sink it in a mold, a metal cup
Spiked on its inner surface like a pineapple.
Half the glass now is regularly dimpled,
And when these dimples are covered with a glaze
Of molten glass they are prisoned air-bubbles,
Breathless, enameled pearly vacancies.

III

I am a person of inflexible habits
And comforting rigidities, and though
I am a twentieth century infidel
From Lawrence, Massachusetts, twice a week
I visit the Cathedral of St. Mark's,
That splendid monument to the labors of
Grave robbers, body snatchers, those lawless two
Entrepreneurial Venetians who
In compliance with the wishes of the Doge
For the greater commercial and religious glory
Of Venice in the year 828
Kidnapped the corpse of the Evangelist
From Alexandria, a sacrilege
The saint seemed to approve. That ancient city
Was drugged and bewildered with an odor of sanctity,
Left powerless and mystified by oils,
Attars and essences of holiness
And roses during the midnight exhumation
And spiriting away of the dead saint
By Buono and his side-kick Rustico—
Goodness in concert with Simplicity
Effecting the major heist of Christendom.

I enter the obscure aquarium dimness,
The movie-palace dark, through which incline
Smoky diagonals and radiant bars
Of sunlight from the high southeastern crescents
Of windowed drums above. Like slow blind fingers
Finding their patient and unvarying way
Across the braille of pavement, edging along
The pavonine and lapidary walls,
Inching through silence as the earth revolves
To huge compulsions, as the turning spheres
Drift in their milky pale galactic light
Through endless quiet, gigantic vacancy,

Unpitying, inhuman, terrible.
In time the eye accommodates itself
To the dull phosphorescence. Gradually
Glories reveal themselves, grave mysteries
Of the faith cast off their shadows, assume their forms
Against a heaven of coined and sequined light,
A splatter of gilt cobblestones, flung grains
Or crumbs of brilliance, the vast open fields
Of the sky turned intimate and friendly. Patines
And laminae, a vermeil shimmering
Of fish-scaled, cataphracted golden plates.
Here are the saints and angels brought together
In studied reveries of happiness.
Enormous wings of seraphim uphold
The crowning domes where the convened apostles
Receive their fiery tongues from the Godhead
Descended to them as a floating dove,
Patriarch and collateral ancestor
Of the pigeons out in the Square. Into those choirs
Of lacquered Thrones, enameled Archangels
And medaled Principalities rise up
A cool plantation of columns, marble shafts
Bearing their lifted pathways, viaducts
And catwalks through the middle realms of heaven.
Even as God descended into the mass
And thick of us, so is He borne aloft
As promise and precursor to us all,
Ascending in the central dome's vast hive
Of honeyed luminosity. Behind
The altar He appears, two fingers raised
In benediction, in what seems two-thirds
Of the Boy Scout salute, wishing us well.
And we are gathered here below the saints,
Virtues and martyrs, sheltered in their glow,
Soothed by the punk and incense, to rejoice
In the warm light of Gabrieli's horns,
And for a moment of unwonted grace

We are so blessed as to forget ourselves.
Perhaps. There is something selfish in the self,
The cell's craving for perpetuity,
The sperm's ignorant hope, the animal's rule
Of haunch and sinew, testicle and groin,
That refers all things whatever, near and far,
To one's own needs or fantasized desires.
Returning suddenly to the chalk-white sunlight
Of out-of-doors, one spots among the tourists
Those dissolute young with heavy-lidded gazes
Of cool, clear-eyed, stony depravity
That in the course of only a few years
Will fade into the terrifying boredom
In the faces of Carpaccio's prostitutes.
From motives that are anything but kindly
I ignore their indiscreet solicitations
And far more obvious poverty. The mind
Can scarcely cope with the world's sufferings,
Must blinker itself to much or else go mad.
And the bargain that we make for our sanity
Is the knowledge that when at length it comes our turn
To be numbered with the outcasts, the maimed, the poor,
The injured and insulted, they will turn away,
The fortunate and healthy, as I turn now
(Though touched as much with compassion as with lust,
Knowing the smallest gift would reverse our roles,
Expose me as weak and thus exploitable.
There is more stamina, twenty times more hope
In the least of them than there is left in me.)
I take my loneliness as a vocation,
A policied exile from the human race,
A cultivated, earned misanthropy
After the fashion of the Miller of Dee.

It wasn't always so. I was an Aid Man,
A Medic with an infantry company,
Who because of my refusal to bear arms

Was constrained to bear the wounded and the dead
From under enemy fire, and to bear witness
To inconceivable pain, usually shot at
Though banded with Red Crosses and unarmed.
There was a corporal I knew in Heavy Weapons,
Someone who carried with him into combat
A book of etiquette by Emily Post.
Most brought with them some token of the past,
Some emblem of attachment or affection
Or coddled childhood—bibles and baby booties,
Harmonicas, love letters, photographs—
But this was different. I discovered later
That he had been brought up in an orphanage,
So the book was his fiction of kindliness,
A novel in which personages of wealth
Firmly secure domestic tranquility.
He'd cite me instances. It seems a boy
Will not put "Mr." on his calling cards
Till he leaves school, and may omit the "Mr."
Even while at college. Bread and butter plates
Are never placed on a formal dinner table.
At a simple dinner party one may serve
Claret instead of champagne with the meat.
The satin facings on a butler's lapels
Are narrower than a gentleman's, and he wears
Black waistcoat with white tie, whereas the gentleman's
White waistcoat goes with both black tie and white.
When a lady lunches alone at her own home
In a formally kept house the table is set
For four. As if three Elijahs were expected.
This was to him a sort of *Corpus Juris,*
An ancient piety and governance
Worthy of constant dream and meditation.
He haunts me here, that seeker after law
In a lawless world, in rainsoaked combat boots,
Oil-stained fatigues and heavy bandoleers.
He was killed by enemy machine-gun fire.

His helmet had fallen off. They had sheared away
The top of his cranium like a soft-boiled egg,
And there he crouched, huddled over his weapon,
His brains wet in the chalice of his skull.

IV

Where to begin? In a heaven of golden serifs
Or smooth and rounded loaves of risen gold,
Formed into formal Caslon capitals
And graced with a pretzeled, sinuous ampersand
Against a sanded ground of fire-truck red,
Proclaiming to the world at large, "The Great
Atlantic & Pacific Tea Co."?
The period alone appeared to me
An eighteen-karat doorknob beyond price.
This was my uncle's store where I was raised.
A shy asthmatic child, I was permitted
To improvise with used potato sacks
Of burlap a divan behind the counter
Where I could lie and read or dream my dreams.
These were infused with the smell of fruit and coffee,
Strong odors of American abundance.
Under the pressed-tin ceiling's coffering
I'd listen to the hissing radiator,
Hung with its can, like a tapped maple tree,
To catch its wrathful spittings, and meditate
On the arcane meaning of the mystic word
(Fixed in white letters backwards on the window)
That referred inscrutably to nothing else
Except itself. An uncracked code: SALADA.
By childhood's rules of inference it concerned
Saladin and the camphors of the East,
And through him, by some cognate lineage
Of sound and mystic pedigree, Aladdin,
A hushed and shadowy world of minarets,
Goldsmiths, persimmons and the ninety-nine
Unutterable Arabian names of God.
I had an eye for cyphers and riddling things.
Of all my schoolmates I was the only one
Who knew that on the bottle of Worcestershire
The conjured names of Lea and Perrins figure

Forty-eight times, weaving around the border
As well as the obvious places front and back.
I became in time a local spelling champion,
Encouraged and praised at home, where emphasis
Was placed on what was then called *elocution*
And upon "building" a vocabulary,
A project that seemed allied to architecture,
The unbuttressed balancing of wooden blocks
Into a Tower of Babel. Still, there were prizes
For papers in my English class: Carlyle
On The Dignity of Labor; John Stuart Mill
On Happiness. But the origin of things
Lies elsewhere. Back in some genetic swamp.

    My uncle had worked hard to get his store.
Soon as he could he brought his younger brothers
From the Old Country. My father brought his bride
Of two months to the second-story room
Above the storage. Everybody shared
Labors and profits; they stayed open late
Seven days a week (but closed on Christmas Day)
And did all right. But cutting up the pie
Of measured earnings among five adults
(Four brothers and my mother—I didn't count,
Being one year old at the time) seemed to my father
A burden upon everyone. He announced
That he was going west to make his fortune
And would send soon as he could for mother and me.
Everyone thought him brave and enterprising.
There was a little party, with songs and tears
And special wine, purchased for the occasion.
He left. We never heard from him again.

    When I was six years old it rained and rained
And never seemed to stop. I had an oilskin,
A bright sou'wester, stiff and sunflower yellow,
And fireman boots. Rain stippled the windows

Of the school bus that brought us home at dusk
That was no longer dusk but massing dark
As that small world of kids drove into winter,
And always in that dark our grocery store
Looked like a theater or a puppet show,
Lit, warm, and peopled with the family cast,
Full of prop vegetables, a brighter sight
Than anyone else's home. Therefore I knew
Something was clearly up when the bus door
Hinged open and all the lights were on upstairs
But only the bulb at the cash register lit
The store itself, half dark, and on the steps,
Still in his apron, standing in the rain,
My uncle. He was soaked through. He told me
He was taking me to a movie and then to supper
At a restaurant, though the next day was school
And I had homework. It was clear to me
That such a treat exacted on my part
The condition that I shouldn't question it.
We went to see a bedroom comedy,
"Let Us Be Gay," scarcely for six-year-olds,
Throughout the length of which my uncle wept.
And then we went to a Chinese restaurant
And sat next to the window where I could see,
Beyond the Chinese equivalent of SALADA
Encoded on the glass, the oil-slicked streets,
The gutters with their little Allagashes
Bent on some urgent mission to the sea.
Next day they told me that my mother was dead.
I didn't go to school. I watched the rain
From the bedroom window or from my burlap nest
Behind the counter. My whole life was changed
Without my having done a single thing.
Perhaps because of those days of constant rain
I am always touched by it now, touched and assuaged.
Perhaps that early vigilance at windows
Explains why I have now come to regard

Life as a spectator sport. But I find peace
In the arcaded dark of the piazza
When a thunderstorm comes up. I watch the sky
Cloud into tarnished zinc, to Quaker gray
Drabness, its shrouded vaults, fog-bound crevasses
Blinking with huddled lightning, and await
The vast *son et lumière*. The city's lamps
Faintly ignite in the gathered winter gloom.
The rumbled thunder starts—an avalanche
Rolling down polished corridors of sound,
Rickety tumbrels blundering across
A stone and empty cellarage. And then,
Like a whisper of dry leaves, the rain begins.
It stains the paving stones, forms a light mist
Of brilliant crystals dulled with tones of lead
Three inches off the ground. Blown shawls of rain
Quiver and luff, veil the cathedral front
In flailing laces while the street lamps hold
Fixed globes of sparkled haze high in the air
And the black pavement runs with wrinkled gold
In pools and wet dispersions, fiery spills
Of liquid copper, of squirming, molten brass.
To give one's whole attention to such a sight
Is a sort of blessedness. No room is left
For antecedence, inference, nuance.
One escapes from all the anguish of this world
Into the refuge of the present tense.
The past is mercifully dissolved, and in
Easy obedience to the gospel's word,
One takes no thought whatever of tomorrow,
The soul being drenched in fine particulars.

V

     Seeing is misbelieving, as may be seen
By the angled stems, like fractured tibias,
Misplaced by water's anamorphosis.
Think of the blonde with the exposed midriff
Who grins as the cross-cut saw slides through her navel,
Or, better, the wobbled clarity of streams,
Their graveled bottoms strewn with casual plunder
Of earthen golds, shark grays, palomino browns
Giddily swimming in and out of focus,
Where, in a passing moment of accession,
One thinks one sees in all that spangled bath,
That tarsial, cosmatesque bespattering,
The anchored floating of a giant trout.
All lenses—the corneal tunic of the eye,
Fine scopes and glazier's filaments—mislead us
With insubstantial visions, like objects viewed
Through crizzled and quarrelled panes of Bull's Eye Glass.
It turned out in the end that John Stuart Mill
Knew even less about happiness than I do,
Who know at last, alas, that it is composed
Of clouded, cataracted, darkened sight,
Merciful blindnesses and ignorance.
Only when paradisal bliss had ended
Was enlightenment vouchsafed to Adam and Eve,
"*And the eyes of them both were opened, and they knew . . .*"
I, for example, though I had lost my parents,
Thought I was happy almost throughout my youth.
Innocent, like Othello in his First Act.
"*I saw 't not, thought it not, it harmed not me.*"
The story I have to tell is only my story
By courtesy of painful inference.
So far as I can tell it, it is true,
Though it has comprised the body of such dreams,
Such broken remnant furnishings of the mind
That my unwilling suspension of disbelief

No longer can distinguish between fact
As something outward, independent, given,
And the enfleshment of disembodied thought,
Some melanotic malevolence of my own.
I know this much for sure : When I was eighteen
My father returned home. In a boxcar, dead.
I learned, or else I dreamed, that heading west
He got no further than Toledo, Ohio,
Where late one night in a vacant parking lot
He was robbed, hit on the head with a quart bottle,
Left bleeding and unconscious and soaked with rum
By a couple of thugs who had robbed a liquor store
And found in my father, besides his modest savings,
A convenient means of diverting the police.
He came to in the hospital, walletless,
Paperless, without identity.
He had no more than a dozen words of English
Which, in hysterical anxiety
Or perhaps from the concussion, evaded him.
The doctors seemed to be equally alarmed
By possible effects of the blow to his head
And by his wild excitability
In a tongue nobody there could understand.
He was therefore transferred for observation
To the State Mental Hospital where he stayed
Almost a year before, by merest chance,
A visitor of Lithuanian background
Heard and identified his Lettish speech,
And it could be determined that he was
In full possession of his faculties,
If of little else, and where he had come from
And all the rest of it. The Toledo police
Then wrote my uncle a letter. Without unduly
Stressing their own casualness in the matter,
They told my uncle where his brother was,
How he had come to be there, and that because
He had no funds or visible means of support

He would be held pending a money order
That should cover at least his transportation home.
They wrote three times. They didn't get an answer.

      The immigrants to Lawrence, Massachusetts,
Were moved as by the vision of Isaiah
To come to the New World, to become new
And enter into a peaceful Commonwealth.
This meant hard work, a scrupulous adoption
Of local ways, endeavoring to please
Clients and neighbors, to become at length,
Despite the ineradicable stigma
Of a thick accent, one like all the rest,
Homogenized and inconspicuous.
So much had the prophetic vision come to.
It would not do at all to have it known
That any member of the family
Had been in police custody, or, worse,
In an asylum. All the kind good will
And friendly custom of the neighborhood
Would be withdrawn at the mere breath of scandal.
Prudence is one of the New England virtues
My uncle was at special pains to learn.
And it paid off, as protestant virtue does,
In cold coin of the realm. Soon he could buy
His own store and take his customers with him
From the A. & P. By the time I was in high school
He and his brothers owned a modest chain
Of little grocery stores and butcher shops.
And he took on as well the unpaid task
Of raising me, making himself my parent,
Forbearing and encouraging and kind.
Or so it seemed. Often in my nightmares
Since then I appear craven and repulsive,
Always soliciting his good opinion
As he had sought that of the neighborhood.
The dead keep their own counsel, let nothing slip

About incarceration, so it was judged
Fitting to have the funeral back home.
Home now had changed. We lived, uncle and I,
In a whole house of our own with a German cook.
The body was laid out in the living room
In a casket lined with tufted tea-rose silk,
Upholstered like a Victorian love-seat.
He had never been so comfortable. He looked
Almost my age, more my age than my uncle's,
Since half his forty years had not been lived,
Had merely passed, like birthdays or the weather.
He was, strangely enough, a total stranger
Who bore a clear family resemblance.
And there was torture in my uncle's face
Such as I did not even see at war.
The flowers were suffocating. It was like drowning.
The day after the burial I enlisted,
And two and a half years later was mustered out
As a Section Eight, mentally unsound.

VI

What is our happiest, most cherished dream
Of paradise? Not harps and fugues and feathers
But rather arrested action, an escape
From time, from history, from evolution
Into the blessèd stasis of a painting :
Those tributes, homages, apotheoses
Figured upon the ceilings of the rich
Wherein some rather boorish-looking count,
With game leg and bad breath, roundly despised
By all of his contemporaries, rises
Into the company of the heavenly host
(A pimpled donor among flawless saints)
Viewed by us proletarians on the floor
From under his thick ham and dangled calf
As he is borne beyond our dark resentment
On puffy quilts and comforters of cloud.
Suspended always at that middle height
In numinous diffusions of soft light,
In mild soft-focus, in the "tinted steam"
Of Turner's visions of reality,
He is established at a pitch of triumph,
That shall not fail him, by the painter's skill.
Yet in its way even the passage of time
Seems to inch toward a vast and final form,
To mimic the grand metastasis of art,
As if all were ordained. As the writ saith :
The fathers (and their brothers) shall eat grapes
And the teeth of the children shall be set on edge.
Ho fatto un fiasco, which is to say,
I've made a sort of bottle of my life,
A frangible and a transparent failure.
My efforts at their best are negative :
A poor attempt not to hurt anyone,
A goal which, in the very nature of things,
Is ludicrous because impossible.

Viscid, contaminate, dynastic wastes
Flood through the dark canals, the underpasses,
Ducts and arterial sluices of my body
As through those gutters of which Swift once wrote :
"Sweepings from Butcher Stalls, Dung, Guts, and Blood,
Drown'd Puppies, stinking Sprats, all drench'd in Mud,
Dead Cats and Turnip-Tops come tumbling down the
        Flood."
At least I pass them on to nobody,
Not having married, or authored any children,
Leading a monkish life of modest means
On a trust fund established by my uncle
In a will of which I am the single heir.
I am not young any more, and not very well,
Subject to nightmares and to certain fevers
The doctors cannot cure. There's a Madonna
Set in an alley shrine near where I live
Whose niche is filled with little votive gifts,
Like cookie molds, of pressed tin eyes and legs
And organs she has mercifully cured.
She is not pretty, she is not high art,
But in my infidel way I'm fond of her—
Saint Mary Paregoric, Comforter.
Were she to cure me, what could I offer her?
The gross, intestinal wormings of the brain?

        A virus's life-span is twenty minutes.
Think of its evolutionary zeal,
Like the hyper-active balance-wheel of a watch,
Busy with swift mutations, trundling through
Its own Silurian epochs in a week;
By fierce ambition and Darwinian wit
Acquiring its immunities against
Our warfares and our plagues of medication.
Blessed be the unseen micro-organisms,
For without doubt they shall inherit the earth.
Their generations shall be as the sands of the sea.

I am the dying host by which they live;
In me they dwell and thrive and have their being.
I am the tapered end of a long line,
The thin and febrile phylum of my family :
Of all my father's brothers the one child.
I wander these by-paths and little squares,
A singular Tyrannosauros Rex,
Sauntering towards extinction, an obsolete
Left-over from a weak *ancien régime*
About to be edged out by upstart germs.
I shall pay out the forfeit with my life
In my own lingering way. Just as my uncle,
Who, my blood tells me on its nightly rounds,
May perhaps be "a little more than kin,"
Has paid the price for his unlawful grief
And bloodless butchery by creating me
His guilty legatee, the beneficiary
Of his money and his crimes.
                              In these late days
I find myself frequently at the window,
Its glass a cooling comfort to my temple.
And I lift up mine eyes, not to the hills
Of which there are not any, but to the clouds.
Here is a sky determined to maintain
The reputation of Tiepolo,
A moving vision of a shapely mist,
Full of the splendor of the insubstantial.
Against a diorama of palest blue
Cloud-curds, cloud-stacks, cloud-bushes sun themselves.
Giant confections, impossible meringues,
Soft coral reefs and powdery tumuli
Pass in august processions and calm herds.
Great stadiums, grandstands and amphitheaters,
The tufted, opulent litters of the gods
They seem; or laundered bunting, well-dressed wigs,
Harvests of milk-white, Chinese peonies
That visibly rebuke our stinginess.

246

For all their ghostly presences, they take on
A colorful nobility at evening.
Off to the east the sky begins to turn
Lilac so pale it seems a mood of gray,
Gradually, like the death of virtuous men.
Streaks of electrum richly underline
The slow, flat-bottomed hulls, those floated lobes
Between which quills and spokes of light fan out
Into carnelian reds and nectarines,
Nearing a citron brilliance at the center,
The searing furnace of the glory hole
That fires and fuses clouds of muscatel
With pencilings of gold. I look and look,
As though I could be saved simply by looking
I, who have never earned my way, who am
No better than a viral parasite,
Or the lees of the Venetian underworld,
Foolish and muddled in my later years,
Who was never even at one time a wise child.

I I I

TWO POEMS BY JOSEPH BRODSKY

VERSIONS BY ANTHONY HECHT

CAPE COD LULLABY

I

The Eastern tip of the Empire dives into night;
Cicadas fall silent over some empty lawn;
On classic pediments inscriptions dim from the sight
As a finial cross darkens and then is gone
Like the nearly empty bottle on the table.
From the empty street's patrol-car a refrain
Of Ray Charles' keyboard tinkles away like rain.

Crawling to a vacant beach from the vast wet
Of ocean, a crab digs into sand laced with sea-lather
And sleeps. A giant clock on a brick tower
Rattles its scissors. The face is drenched with sweat.
The street lamps glisten in the stifling weather,
Formally spaced,
Like white shirt buttons open to the waist.

It's stifling. The eye's guided by a blinking stop-light
In its journey to the whiskey across the room
On the night-stand. The heart stops dead a moment, but its
    dull boom
Goes on, and the blood, on pilgrimage gone forth,
Comes back to a crossroad. The body, like an upright,
Rolled-up road-map, lifts an eyebrow in the North.

It's strange to think of surviving, but that's what happened.
Dust settles on furnishings, and a car bends length
Around corners in spite of Euclid. And the deepened
Darkness makes up for the absence of people, of voices,
And so forth, and alters them, by its cunning and strength,
Not to deserters, to ones who have taken flight,
But rather to those now disappeared from sight.

Cape Cod Lullaby

It's stifling. And the thick leaves' rasping sound
Is enough all by itself to make you sweat.
What seems to be a small dot in the dark
Could only be one thing—a star. On the deserted ground
Of a basketball court a vagrant bird has set
Its fragile egg in the steel hoop's ravelled net.
There's a smell of mint now, and of mignonette.

II

Like a despotic Sheik, who can be untrue
To his vast seraglio and multiple desires
Only with a harem altogether new,
Varied and numerous, I have switched Empires.
A step dictated by the acrid, live
Odor of burning carried on the air
From all four quarters (a time for silent prayer!)
And, from the crow's high vantage point, from five.

Like a snake charmer, like the Pied Piper of old,
Playing my flute I passed the green janissaries,
My testes sensing their pole axe's sinister cold,
As when one wades into water. And then with the brine
Of sea-water sharpness filling, flooding the mouth,
I crossed the line

And sailed into muttony clouds. Below me curled
Serpentine rivers, roads bloomed with dust, ricks yellowed,
And everywhere in that diminished world,
In formal opposition, near and far,
Lined up like print in a book about to close,
Armies rehearsed their games in balanced rows
And cities all went dark as caviar.

And then the darkness thickened. All lights fled,
A turbine droned, a head ached rhythmically,
And space backed up like a crab, time surged ahead
Into first place, and streaming westwardly,
Seemed to be heading home, void of all light,
Soiling its garments with the tar of night.

I fell asleep. When I awoke to the day,
Magnetic north had strengthened its deadly pull.
I beheld new heavens, I beheld the earth made new.
It lay
Turning to dust, as flat things always do.

III

Being itself the essence of all things,
Solitude teaches essentials. How gratefully the skin
Receives the leathery coolness of its chair.
Meanwhile my arm, off in the dark somewhere,
Goes wooden in sympathetic brotherhood
With the chair's listless arm of oaken wood.
A glowing oaken grain
Covers the tiny bones of the joints. And the brain
Knocks like the glass's ice-cube tinkling.

It's stifling. On a pool hall's steps, in a dim glow,
Somebody striking a match rescues his face
Of an old black man from the enfolding dark
For a flaring moment. The white-toothed portico
Of the District Courthouse sinks in the thickened lace
Of foliage, and awaits the random search
Of passing headlights. High up on its perch,

Like the fiery warning at Belshazzar's Feast,
The inscription, *Coca-Cola*, hums in red.
In the Country Club's unweeded flowerbed
A fountain whispers its secrets. Unable to rouse
A simple *tirra lirra* in these dull boughs,
A strengthless breeze rustles the tattered, creased
News of the world, its obsolete events,
Against an improvised, unlikely fence

Of iron bedsteads. It's stifling. Leaning on his rifle,
The Unknown Soldier grows even more unknown.
Against a concrete jetty, in dull repose
A trawler scrapes the rusty bridge of its nose.
A weary, buzzing ventilator mills
The U.S.A.'s hot air with metal gills.

Like a carried-over number in addition,
The sea comes up in the dark
And on the beach it leaves its delible mark,
And the unvarying, diastolic motion,
The repetitious, drugged sway of the ocean
Cradles a splinter adrift for a million years.
If you step sideways off the pier's
Edge, you'll continue to fall toward those tides
For a long, long time, your hands stiff at your sides,
But you will make no splash.

IV

The change of Empires is intimately tied
To the hum of words, the soft, fricative spray
Of spittle in the act of speech, the whole
Sum of Lobachevsky's angles, the strange way
That parallels may unwittingly collide
By casual chance some day
As longitudes contrive to meet at the pole.

And the change is linked as well to the chopping of wood,
To the tattered lining of life turned inside out
And thereby changed to a garment dry and good
(To tweed in winter, linen in a heat spell)
And the brain's kernel hardening in its shell.

In general, of all our organs the eye
Alone retains its elasticity,
Pliant, adaptive as a dream or wish.
For the change of Empires is linked with far-flung sight,
With the long gaze cast across the ocean's tide
(Somewhere within us lives a dormant fish)
And the mirror's revelation that the part in your hair
That you meticulously placed on the left side
Mysteriously shows up on the right,

Linked to weak gums, to heartburn brought about
By a diet unfamiliar and alien,
To the intense blankness, to the pristine white
Of the mind, which corresponds to the plain, small
Blank page of letterpaper on which you write.
But now the giddy pen
Points out resemblances, for after all,

The device in your hand is the same old pen and ink
As before, the woodland plants exhibit no change
Of leafage, and the same old bombers range
The clouds toward who knows what
Precisely chosen, carefully targeted spot.
And what you really need now is a drink.

V

New England towns seem much as if they were cast
Ashore along its coastline, beached by a flood-
Tide, and shining in darkness mile after mile

With imbricate, speckled scales of shingle and tile,
Like schools of sleeping fish hauled in by the vast
Nets of a continent that was first discovered
By herring and by cod. But neither cod

Nor herring have had any noble statues raised
In their honor, even though the memorial date
Could be comfortably omitted. As for the great
Flag of the place, it bears no blazon or mark
Of the first fish-founder among its parallel bars,
And as Louis Sullivan might perhaps have said,
Seen in the dark,
It looks like a sketch of towers thrust among stars.

Stifling. A man on his porch has wound a towel
Around his throat. A pitiful, small moth
Batters the window screen and bounces off
Like a bullet that Nature has zeroed in on itself
From an invisible ambush,
Aiming for some improbable bullseye
Right smack in the middle of July.

Because watches keep ticking, pain washes away
With the years. If time picks up the knack
Of panacea, it's because time can't abide
Being rushed, or finally turns insomniac.
And walking or swimming, the dreams of one hemisphere
     (heads)
Swarm with the nightmares, the dark, sinister play
Of its opposite (tails), its double, its underside.

Stifling. Great motionless plants. A distant bark.
A nodding head now jerks itself upright
To keep faces and phone numbers from sliding into the dark
And off the precarious edge of memory.
In genuine tragedy

It's not the fine hero that finally dies, it seems,
But, from constant wear and tear, night after night,
The old stage set itself, giving way at the seams.

VI

Since it's too late by now to say "goodbye"
And expect from time and space any reply
Except an echo that sounds like "here's your tip,"
Pseudo-majestic, cubing every chance
Word that escapes the lip,
I write in a sort of trance,

I write these words out blindly, the scrivening hand
Attempting to outstrip
By a second the "how come?"
That at any moment might escape the lip,
The same lip of the writer,
And sail away into night, there to expand
By geometrical progress, *und so weiter*.

I write from an Empire whose enormous flanks
Extend beneath the sea. Having sampled two
Oceans as well as continents, I feel that I know
What the globe itself must feel: there's nowhere to go.
Elsewhere is nothing more than a far-flung strew
Of stars, burning away.

Better to use a telescope to see
A snail self-sealed to the underside of a leaf.
I always used to regard "infinity"
As the art of splitting a liter into three
Equal components with a couple of friends
Without a drop left over. Not, through a lens,
An aggregate of miles without relief.

Night. A cuckoo wheezes in the Waldorf-
Inglorious. The legions close their ranks
And, leaning against cohorts, sleep upright.
Circuses pile against fora. High in the night
Above the bare blue-print of an empty court,
Like a lost tennis-ball, the moon regards its court,
A chess queen's dream, spare, parqueted, formal and bright.
There's no life without furniture.

VII

Only a corner cordoned off and laced
By dusty cobwebs may properly be called
Right-angled; only after the musketry of applause
And "bravos" does the actor rise from the dead;
Only when the fulcrum is solidly placed
Can a person lift, by Archimedian laws,
The weight of this world. And only that body whose weight
Is balanced at right angles to the floor
Can manage to walk about and navigate.

Stifling. There's a cockroach mob in the stadium
Of the zinc washbasin, crowding around the old
Corpse of a dried-up sponge. Turning its crown,
A bronze faucet, like Caesar's laureled head,
Deposes upon the living and the dead
A merciless column of water in which they drown.

The little bubble-beads inside my glass
Look like the holes in cheese.
No doubt that gravity holds sway,
Just as upon a solid mass,
Over such small transparencies as these.
And its accelerating waterfall
(Thirty-two feet per sec. per sec.) refracts
As does a ray of light in human clay.

Only the stacked, white china on the stove
Could look so much like a squashed, collapsed pagoda.
Space lends itself just to repeatable things,
Roses, for instance. If you see one alone,
You instantly see two. The bright corona,
The crimson petals abuzz, acrawl with wings
Of dragonflies, of wasps and bees with stings.

Stifling. Even the shadow on the wall,
Servile and weak as it is, still mimics the rise
Of the hand that wipes the forehead's sweat. The smell
Of old body is even clearer now
Than body's outline. Thought loses its defined
Edges, and the frazzled mind
Goes soft in its soup-bone skull. No one is here
To set the proper focus of your eyes.

VIII

Preserve these words against a time of cold,
A day of fear : Man survives like a fish,
Stranded, beached, but intent
On adapting itself to some deep, cellular wish,
Wriggling toward bushes, forming hinged leg-struts, then
To depart (leaving a track like the scrawl of a pen)
For the interior, the heart of the continent.

Full-breasted sphinxes there are, and lions winged
Like fanged and mythic birds.
Angels in white, as well, and nymphs of the sea.
To one who shoulders the vast obscurity
Of darkness and heavy heat (may one add, grief?)
They are more cherished than the concentric, ringed
Zeroes that ripple outwards from dropped words.

Even space itself, where there's nowhere to sit down,
Declines, like a star in its ether, its cold sky.
Yet just because shoes exist and the foot is shod
Some surface will always be there, some place to stand,
A portion of dry land.
And its brinks and beaches will be enchanted by
The soft song of the cod :

"Time is far greater than space. Space is a thing.
Whereas time is, in essence, the thought, the conscious dream
Of a thing. And life itself is a variety
Of time. The carp and bream
Are its clots and distillates. As are even more stark
And elemental things, including the sea-
Wave and the firmament of the dry land.
Including death, that punctuation mark.

At times, in that chaos, that piling up of days,
The sound of a single word rings in the ear,
Some brief, syllabic cry,
Like 'love,' perhaps, or possibly merely 'hi!'
But before I can make it out, static or haze
Trouble the scanning lines that undulate
And wave like the loosened ripples of your hair."

IX

Man broods over his life like night above a lamp.
At certain moments a thought takes leave of one
Of the brain's hemispheres, and slips, as a bedsheet might,
From under the restless sleeper's body-clamp,
Revealing who-knows-what-under-the-sun.
Unquestionably, night

Is a bulky thing, but not so infinite
As to engross both lobes. By slow degrees
The africa of the brain, its europe, the asian mass of it,
As well as other prominences in its crowded seas,
Creaking on their axis, turn a wrinkled cheek
Toward the electric heron with its lightbulb of a beak.

Behold: Aladdin says "Sesame!" and presto! there's a golden
    trove.
Caesar calls for his Brutus down the dark forum's colonnades.
In the jade pavilion a nightingale serenades
The Mandarin on the delicate theme of love.
A young girl rocks a cradle in the lamp's arena of light.
A naked Papuan leg keeps up a boogie-woogie beat.

Stifling. And so, cold knees tucked snug against the night,
It comes to you all at once, there in the bed,
That this is marriage. That beyond the customs sheds
Across dozens of borders there turns upon its side
A body you now share nothing with, unless
It be the ocean's bottom, hidden from sight,
And the experience of nakedness.

Nevertheless, you won't get up together.
Because, while it may be light way over there,
The dark still governs in your hemisphere.
One solar source has never been enough
To serve two average bodies, not since the time
God glued the world together in its prime.
The light has never been enough.

X

I notice a sleeve's hem, as my eyes fall,
And an elbow bending itself. Coordinates show
My location as paradise, that sovereign, blessed

Place where all purpose and longing is set at rest.
This is a planet without vistas, with no
Converging lines, with no prospects at all.

Touch the table-corner, touch the sharp nib of the pen
With your fingertip : you can tell such things could hurt.
And yet the paradise of the inert
Resides in pointedness;
Whereas in the lives of men
It is fleeting, a misty, mutable excess
That will not come again.

I find myself, as it were, on a mountain peak.
Beyond me there is . . . Chronos and thin air.
Preserve these words. The paradise men seek
Is a dead end, a worn-out, battered cape
Bent into crooked shape,
A cone, a finial cap, a steel ship's bow
From which the lookout never shouts "Land Ho!"

All you can tell for certain is the time.
That said, there's nothing left but to police
The revolving hands. The eye drowns silently
In the clock-face as in a broad, bottomless sea.
In paradise all clocks refuse to chime
For fear they might, in striking, disturb the peace.

Double all absences, multiply by two
Whatever's missing, and you'll have some clue
To what it's like here. A number, in any case,
Is also a word and, as such, a device
Or gesture that melts away without a trace,
Like a small cube of ice.

XI

Great issues leave a trail of words behind,
Free-form as clouds of tree-tops, rigid as dates
Of the year. So too, decked out in a paper hat,
The body viewing the ocean. It is selfless, flat
As a mirror as it stands in the darkness there.
Upon its face, just as within its mind,
Nothing but spreading ripples anywhere.

Consisting of love, of dirty words, a blend
Of ashes, the fear of death, the fragile case
Of the bone, and the groin's jeopardy, an erect
Body at sea-side is the foreskin of space,
Letting semen through. His cheek tear-silver-flecked,
Man juts forth into Time; man is his own end.

The Eastern end of the Empire dives into night—
Throat-high in darkness. The coil of the inner ear,
Like a snail's helix, faithfully repeats
Spirals of words in which it seems to hear
A voice of its own, and this tends to incite
The vocal chords, but it doesn't help you see.
In the realm of Time, no precipice creates
An echo's formal, answering symmetry.

Stifling. Only when lying flat on your back
Can you launch, with a sigh, your dry speech toward those
     mute,
Infinite regions above. With a soft sigh.
But the thought of the land's vastness, your own minute
Size in comparison, swings you forth and back
From wall to wall, like a cradle's rock-a-bye.

Therefore, sleep well. Sweet dreams. Knit up that sleeve.
Sleep as those only do who have gone pee-pee.
Countries get snared in maps, never shake free

Of their net of latitudes. Don't ask who's there
If you think the door is creaking. Never believe
The person who might reply and claim he's there.

XII

The door is creaking. A cod stands at the sill.
He asks for a drink, naturally, for God's sake.
You can't refuse a traveler a nip.
You indicate to him which road to take,
A winding highway, and wish him a good trip.
He takes his leave, but his identical

Twin has got a salesman's foot in the door.
(The two fish are as duplicate as glasses.)
All night a school of them come visiting.
But people who make their homes along the shore
Know how to sleep, have learned how to ignore
The measured tread of these approaching masses.

Sleep. The land beyond you is not round.
It is merely long, with various dip and mound,
Its ups and downs. Far longer is the sea.
At times, like a wrinkled forehead, it displays
A rolling wave. And longer still than these
Is the strand of matching beads of countless days;

And nights; and beyond these, the blindfold mist,
Angels in paradise, demons down in hell.
And longer a hundredfold than all of this
Are the thoughts of life, the solitary thought
Of death. And ten times that, longer than all,
The queer, vertiginous thought of Nothingness.

But the eye can't see that far. In fact, it must
Close down its lid to catch a glimpse of things.
Only this way—in sleep—can the eye adjust
To proper vision. Whatever may be in store,
For good or ill, in the dreams that such sleep brings
Depends on the sleeper. A cod stands at the door.

LAGOON

I

Down in the lobby three elderly women, bored,
Take up, with their knitting, the Passion of Our Lord
      As the universe and the tiny realm
Of the *pension* "*Accademia*," side by side,
With TV blaring, sail into Christmastide,
      A look out desk-clerk at the helm.

II

And a nameless lodger, a nobody, boards the boat,
A bottle of grappa concealed in his raincoat
      As he gains his shadowy room, bereaved
Of memory, homeland, son, with only the noise
Of distant forests to grieve for his former joys,
      If anyone is grieved.

III

Venetian churchbells, tea cups, mantle clocks,
Chime and confound themselves in this stale box
      Of assorted lives. The brazen, coiled
Octopus-chandelier appears to be licking,
In a triptych mirror, bedsheet and mattress ticking,
      Sodden with tears and passion-soiled.

IV

Blown by nightwinds, an Adriatic tide
Floods the canals, boats rock from side to side,
      Moored cradles, and the humble bream,
Not ass and oxen, guards the rented bed
Where the windowblind above your sleeping head
      Moves to the sea-star's guiding beam.

V

So this is how we cope, putting out the heat
Of grappa with nightstand water, carving the meat
      Of flounder instead of Christmas roast,
So that Thy earliest back-boned ancestor
Might feed and nourish us, O Savior,
      This winter night on a damp coast.

VI

A Christmas without snow, tinsel or tree,
At the edge of a map-and-land corseted sea;
      Having scuttled and sunk its scallop shell,
Concealing its face while flaunting its backside,
Time rises from the goddess's frothy tide,
      Yet changes nothing but clock-hand and bell.

VII

A drowning city, where suddenly the dry
Light of reason dissolves in the moisture of the eye;
      Its winged lion, that can read and write,

Southern kin of northern Sphinxes of renown,
Won't drop his book and holler, but calmly drown
      In splinters of mirror, splashing light.

VIII

The gondola knocks against its moorings. Sound
Cancels itself, hearing and words are drowned,
      As is that nation where among
Forests of hands the tyrant of the State
Is voted in, its only candidate,
      And spit goes ice-cold on the tongue.

IX

So let us place the left paw, sheathing its claws,
In the crook of the arm of the other one, because
      This makes a hammer-and-sickle sign
With which to salute our era and bestow
A mute *Up Yours Even Unto The Elbow*
      Upon the nightmares of our time.

X

The raincoated figure is settling into place
Where Sophia, Constance, Prudence, Faith and Grace
      Lack futures, the only tense that is
Is present, where either a goyish or yiddish kiss
Tastes bitter, like the city, where footsteps fade
      Invisibly along the colonnade,

XI

Trackless and blank as a gondola's passage through
A water surface, smoothing out of view
      The measured wrinkles of its path,
Unmarked as a broad "So long!" like the wide piazza's space,
Or as a cramped "I love," like the narrow alleyways,
      Erased and without aftermath.

XII

Moldings and carvings, palaces and flights
Of stairs. Look up : the lion smiles from heights
      Of a tower wrapped as in a coat
Of wind, unbudged, determined not to yield,
Like a rank weed at the edge of a plowed field,
      And girdled round by Time's deep moat.

XIII

Night in St. Mark's piazza. A face as creased
As a finger from its fettering ring released,
      Biting a nail, is gazing high
Into that *nowhere* of pure thought, where sight
Is baffled by the bandages of night,
      Serene, beyond the naked eye,

Lagoon

XIV

Where, past all boundaries and all predicates,
Black, white or colorless, vague, volatile states,
      Something, some object, comes to mind.
Perhaps a body. In our dim days and few,
The speed of light equals a fleeting view,
      Even when blackout robs us blind.

NOTES

PAGE 188 "The Deodand." Deodand is defined as "A thing forfeited or to be given to God; *spec.* in *Eng. Law,* a personal chattel which, having been the immediate occasion of the death of a human being, was given to God as an expiatory offering, i.e., forfeited to the Crown to be applied to pious uses. . . ." The poem is based on a painting by Pierre-Auguste Renoir, called *Parisians Dressed in Algerian Costume,* in the National Museum of Western Art, Tokyo.

PAGE 190 The concluding lines in French may be rendered:

> *Let me be given nourishment at your hands*
> *Since it's for you I perform my little dance.*
> *For I am the street-walker, Magdalen,*
> *And come the dawn I'll be on my way again,*
> *The beauty queen, Miss France.*

PAGE 195 "Such was this place, a hapless rural seat": cf. *Paradise Lost,* Bk. iv, 11.246–7.

PAGE 200 "Which also happens to be the word for bitter": strictly speaking it is the adverbial "bitterly," but this lapse is to be explained by the imperfect memory of a former student in an hour of stress.

PAGE 202 "Shiva": Hindu god of destruction, associated with dancing and with fire.

PAGE 204 Ronsard, Bk. ii, Ode XIV

PAGE 208 Horace, Bk. i, Ode i

PAGE 213 "REM" Rapid Eye Movement—a physiological indicator that a sleeper is dreaming.

PAGE 217 Horace, Bk. i, Ode v

PAGE 227 "Of Byron writing, 'Many a fine day'": "I should, many a good day, have blown my brains out, but for the recollection that it would have given pleasure to my mother-in-law . . ." From a letter to Tom Moore, January 28, 1817.

PAGE 228 "Byron confessed to: 'If I should reach old age'": "But I feel something, which makes me think that if I ever reach near to old age, like Swift, I shall die at 'top' first." From a diary of 1821. Once, pointing at a lightning-blasted oak, Swift had said to Edward Young, about his apprehensions of approaching madness, "I shall be like that tree. I shall die first at the top."

PAGE 229 "Young Henry Fuseli, . ." Johann Heinrich Füssli, later known as John Henry Fuseli, born in Zurich, February 6, 1741, died in London, April 16, 1825. Ordained a Zwinglian minister in 1761, but abandoned the ministry, first for literature and later for painting. Settled in London in 1779, where he was elected to the Royal Academy in 1790. He was a friend of Blake, and *The Nightmare* is probably his best-known painting.

PAGE 233   "Miller of Dee":

> *There was a jolly miller once,*
>   *Lived on the river Dee;*
> *He worked and sang from morn till night,*
>   *No lark more blithe than he.*

> *And this the burden of his song*
>   *Forever used to be—*
> *I care for nobody, no, not I,*
>   *And nobody cares for me.*

PAGE 245   "As through those gutters of which Swift once wrote": "A Description of a City Shower," Oct. 1710.

PAGE 253   "I beheld new heavens, I beheld the earth made new" is an ironic echo of Isaiah 65:17—"For, behold, I create new heavens, and a new earth; and the former shall not be remembered, nor come into mind." The blessedness of being allowed to forget the old and ruined life is clearly connected in this poem with getting drunk.

PAGES 259   "Preserve these words," a phrase which occurs both in Section VIII and Section X, is an echo of a Mandelstam poem, addressed and dedicated to Anna Akhmatova, which, in the translation by Clarence Brown and W. S. Merwin, begins, "Keep my words forever for their aftertaste of misfortune and smoke."

PAGE 268   "northern Sphinxes": sculptured figures placed along the embankments of the Neva River in St. Petersburg.

A Note About the Author

ANTHONY HECHT's first book of poems, *A Summoning of Stones*, appeared in 1954. He is also the author of *The Hard Hours*, which won the Pulitzer Prize for poetry in 1968, of *Millions of Strange Shadows*, 1977, and of *The Venetian Vespers*, 1979. He is the translator (with Helen Bacon) of Aeschylus' *Seven Against Thebes*, 1973, and coeditor (with John Hollander) in 1967 of a volume of light verse, *Jiggery-Pokery*. A collection of his critical essays, *Obbligati*, was published in 1986. He has received the Bollingen Prize in Poetry, the Librex-Guggenheim Eugenio Montale Award and is presently University Professor in the Graduate School of Georgetown University.

A Note on the Type

The text of this book was set in a typeface called WALBAUM, named for Justus Erich Walbaum (1768–1839), a typefounder who removed from his beginnings in Goslar to Weimar in 1803. It is likely that he produced this famous type face shortly thereafter, following the designs of the French typefounder, Firmin Didot. His original matrices are still in existence, owned by the Berthold foundry of Berlin. Continuously popular in Germany since its inception, the face was introduced to England by the Monotype Corporation in 1934, and has steadily grown in popularity ever since.

Composition by Graphic Composition, Inc., Athens, Georgia
Printed and bound by Halliday Lithographers, West Hanover, Massachusetts
Designed by Harry Ford